LIVING ABOVE THE LEVEL OF MEDIOCRITY

A Commitment to Excellence

BIBLE STUDY GUIDE

From the Bible-teaching ministry of

Charles R. Swindoll

INSIGHT FOR LIVING

Chuck graduated in 1963 from Dallas Theological Seminary, where he now serves as the school's fourth president, helping to prepare a new generation of men and women for the ministry. Chuck has served in pastorates in three states: Massachusetts, Texas, and California, including almost twenty-three years at the First Evangelical Free Church in Fullerton, California. His sermon messages have been aired over radio since 1979 as the *Insight for Living* broadcast. A best-selling author, Chuck has written numerous books and booklets on many subjects.

Based on the outlines and transcripts of Chuck's sermons, the study guide text is coauthored by Ken Gire, a graduate of Texas Christian University and Dallas Theological Seminary. The Living Insights are written by Ken Gire and Bill Butterworth, a graduate of Florida Bible College, Dallas Theological Seminary, and Florida Atlantic University.

Editor in Chief: Cynthia Swindoll
Coauthor of Text: Ken Gire
Authors of Living Insights: Bill Butterworth, Ken Gire
Assistant Editor: Wendy Peterson
Copy Editors: Deborah Gibbs, Cheryl Gilmore, Karene Wells
Designer: Gary Lett
Publishing System Specialist: Bob Haskins
Director, Communications and Marketing Division: Deedee Snyder
Marketing Manager: Alene Cooper
Project Coordinator: Colette Muse
Production Manager: John Norton

ISBN 1-57972-089-7
COVER PHOTOGRAPH: Art Wolfe/Allstock, Inc.
Printed in the United States of America

Contents

RESISTING MEDIOCRITY INCLUDES STANDING COURAGEOUSLY

*This message was not a part of the original series but is compatible with it.

INTRODUCTION

The trackless path of an eagle in high flight never fails to seize our attention. "The way of an eagle in the sky" is one of those sights Solomon of old acclaimed as being "too wonderful for me" (Prov. 30:18–19). The soaring eagle represents healthy independence, unintimidated courage, strong confidence, and an almost invincible determination to be different from the majority. Everyone admires those eaglelike qualities.

God never planned for His people to become submerged in the slimy swamp of status quo existence. On the contrary, He is pleased to have us soar, living our lives far above the level of mediocrity. This does not mean that we shall always enjoy great success or be financially prosperous or continually healthy or free from the demands and difficulties of humanity. But it *does* mean that we can counteract the gravity pull of discouragement and defeat.

My sincere desire is that you will find an enormous boost of encouragement in these pages . . . that you will catch a glimpse of hope which results in a fresh commitment to excellence. There is no better way to live! As Isaac D'Israeli once wrote, ". . . it is a wretched taste to be gratified with mediocrity when the excellent lies before us."

Chuck Swindoll

PUTTING TRUTH INTO ACTION

Knowledge apart from application falls short of God's desire for His children. He wants us to apply what we learn so that we will change and grow. This study guide was prepared with these goals in mind. As you go through the following pages, we hope your desire to discover biblical truth will grow as your understanding of God's Word increases and that you will be encouraged to apply what you've learned.

To assist you in your study, we've included a section called **Living Insights** at the end of each lesson. These exercises will challenge you to study further and to think of specific ways to put your discoveries into action.

There are many ways to use this guide—in personal devotions, group studies, discussions with friends and family, and Sunday school classes. And, of course, it's an ideal study aid when you're listening to its corresponding "Insight for Living" radio series.

To benefit most from this study guide, we would encourage you to consider it a spiritual journal. That's why we've included space in the **Living Insights** for recording your thoughts and discoveries. We hope you'll return to those sections often for review and encouragement as you continue to grow in your walk with Christ.

Ken Gire

Ken Gire
Coauthor of Text
Author of Living Insights

LIVING ABOVE THE LEVEL OF MEDIOCRITY

A Commitment to Excellence

Part One

Confronting Mediocrity Takes Thinking Clearly

Chapter 1

It Starts in Your Mind

(PART ONE)

Ephesians 6:10–12; 2 Corinthians 2:10–11; 10:3–5

December 7, 1941. The island of Oahu, Hawaii. Sunrise: 6:26 A.M.

It was a picture-perfect, postcard morning. Light northeast trade winds played over the peaceful Pacific harbor as an armada of cumulus clouds sailed proudly overhead. The U.S. sailors stationed there yawned and stretched to greet the lazy Sunday morning. This idyllic setting seemed the least likely place in all the earth for a war to start, but at five minutes till eight, the calm blanketing Pearl Harbor was slashed by the ruthless propellers of enemy warplanes.

In a carefully planned strategy, 190 Japanese planes from six aircraft carriers swooped down from the cloud cover, diving to make their attack in coordinated waves of strafing and bombing. Around the island, twenty-five submarines waited to pick off survivors of the air attack, while several two-man subs infiltrated the harbor to finish off the crippled U.S. fleet.

When the enemy strike force returned to the carriers and the smoke of battle cleared, 2,330 servicemen were dead, another 1,145 wounded.

The enemy's strategy had been meticulously planned, carefully coordinated, and almost flawlessly executed. With a loss of only twenty-nine planes, five midget submarines, and fewer than one hundred men, the Japanese had sunk five U.S. battleships, demolished two destroyers and blown the bow off a third, while putting many other warships permanently or temporarily out of commission.

As a Christian, you wake up to a Pearl Harbor of your own every morning. But it doesn't take place on an island in the Pacific. Your enemy sets his sights on the small harbor where your thoughts, beliefs, and attitudes are serenely docked, tied to their moorings, seemingly safe. On any day, Satan can launch a surprise attack that within minutes can torpedo your testimony, char your character, and sink your spiritual life.

The Schemes of Satan

The warning Peter gives us concerning Satan reveals something of this enemy's strategy.

> Be of sober spirit, be on the alert. Your adversary, the devil, prowls about like a roaring lion, seeking someone to devour. (1 Pet. 5:8)

Satan is both relentless and ruthless. He not only *prowls;* he also *devours*. Consequently, you should keep your eyes peeled to his wanderings and your ears perked to his roarings. Once he is sighted, you should brace yourself for an attack.

> Put on the full armor of God, that you may be able to stand firm against the schemes of the devil. (Eph. 6:11)

The word *schemes* in verse 11 is transliterated *methodeia* in the Greek. From this we get our word *method*. If the devil is our adversary as 1 Peter 5:8 says, it stands to reason he will attack us. If he will attack us, it further stands to reason that he will have a plan of attack—a scheme, a strategy. And that strategy is not always a frontal assault, direct and easy to recognize; most often it's subtle, infiltrating another realm entirely, as the apostle Paul reveals.

> For our struggle is not against flesh and blood, but against the rulers, against the powers, against the world forces of this darkness, against the spiritual forces of wickedness in the heavenly places. (Eph. 6:12)

Whether between nations or neighbors, battles on earth are only muted shadows cast from a larger spiritual battlefield—"the spiritual forces of wickedness in the heavenly places." The spiritual battle is our real struggle. That's where eternity is won or lost—not at the Battle of the Bulge or at Normandy or Pearl Harbor.

However, because the spiritual battle is invisible and, therefore, often inconspicuous, we are sometimes ignorant of it altogether. It is for this reason that, in 2 Corinthians 2, Paul frankly warns the church to forgive a repentant sinner and reaffirm their love for him "in order that no advantage be taken of us by Satan; for we are not ignorant of his *schemes*" (v. 11, emphasis added). This word *schemes* differs from the one used in Ephesians 6:11. Here it means "thought" or "mind."[1] To paraphrase, we could say that *we are not ignorant of the fact that Satan has his sights set on our minds*.

His strategy, then, is to get to our minds . . . to lull us into mediocrity . . . to blunt the edges of our thinking . . . to cloud our reasoning. He knows the truth of the proverb "as [a man] thinks within himself, so he is" (Prov. 23:7a).

The Stronghold of the Mind

Because the battle raging around us is unseen, visual aids are necessary. In 2 Corinthians 10:3–5, Paul helps us see the real war by putting a transparency on our overhead projector.

> For though we walk in the flesh, we do not war according to the flesh, for the weapons of our warfare are not of the flesh, but divinely powerful for the destruction of fortresses. We are destroying speculations and every lofty thing raised up against the knowledge of God, and we are taking every thought captive to the obedience of Christ.

In this illustration, Paul compares the mind to a fortress. Our minds were enemy-held territories in our unsaved days—Satan's base of operations, his stronghold. When we came to know Christ, though, our allegiance changed and a new power of life took charge. Satan was out; Christ was in.

However, our adversary doesn't give up "his turf" so easily. He has wall-like thought patterns in place, as well as "lofty" mental blocks against spiritual viewpoints. So after we have planted Christ's flag in the fortress of our minds, the Holy Spirit comes in to repattern our whole way of thinking to align it with the mind of Christ. And He is engaged in this battle constantly.

Is every one of your thoughts captive to the obedience of Christ? Or do you have some that continue to bolt and run amok through your mind? If you have to keep dragging those willful thoughts back by the scruff of their necks, kicking and screaming, I'd like to suggest a strategy that will not only keep them behind bars but also reform them into law-abiding citizens.

1. The Greek word is *noēma*.

The Strategy for Spiritual Victory

Since Satan schemes to storm the stronghold of our minds, we must forge a strategy on the anvil of God's Word to combat his attacks. David, a great military leader accustomed to poring over battle maps, provides us with a simple yet profound plan to win the battle for the mind.

> Thy word I have treasured in my heart,
> That I may not sin against Thee. (Ps. 119:11)

In the following chapter, we will learn how to equip ourselves to mount a major counterattack against Satan by memorizing, personalizing, and analyzing the Word of God.

A Concluding Thought

Of the eighteen U.S. warships sunk or damaged at Pearl Harbor, thirteen were repaired to later launch a counterattack on the Japanese fleet. Of the six aircraft carriers from that Japanese strike force, four were sunk 180 days later in the Battle of Midway, and only a single destroyer survived the war. The war ended 1,364 days after it started, in crushing defeat for those who started it. And it ended on the deck of a U.S. battleship—not in Pearl Harbor, but in Tokyo Bay.

In the past, Satan may have made some devastating strikes on your mind. But like the Pacific fleet, those thoughts can be not only restored but also mobilized in a counteroffensive against the enemy. If you treasure God's Word in your heart, then, thought by thought, the battle for your mind will be won.

Living Insights — STUDY ONE

Satan is indeed a cunning strategist. In what many consider to be C. S. Lewis' most famous work, *The Screwtape Letters*, the author created a correspondence between an elderly devil, Screwtape, and his young nephew Wormwood. Screwtape's fictitious counsel to the eager Wormwood reveals something of the true schemes of Satan.

> You will say that these are very small sins; and doubtless, like all young tempters, you are anxious to be able to report spectacular wickedness. But do remember, the only thing that matters is the extent

> to which you separate the man from the Enemy. It does not matter how small the sins are, provided that their cumulative effect is to edge the man away from the Light and out into the Nothing. Murder is no better than cards if cards can do the trick. Indeed, the safest road to Hell is the gradual one—the gentle slope, soft underfoot, without sudden turnings, without milestones, without signposts.[2]

Is there something in your life that is distancing you from God—inching you away from the light? It may be something small. It may be something good—even religious. Take some time now to bring it out of its dark hiding place by writing it down.

How does this subtle something take you away from God? What is it softly whispering to your mind?

In the days to come, train your inner ears to listen for Satan's scheming. He may use something on you that's barely detectable. But if it's a wedge, it will put an empty space between you and the Lord.

Living Insights STUDY TWO

We tend to be shaped by what our minds think about most often. If we always think about ourselves, we stand a good chance of becoming egoists. If we think about material things all the time, we'll most likely become materialistic. If we brood over our fears, doubtless we'll grow paranoid; if on others' wrongs, we'll become bitter.

2. C. S. Lewis, *The Screwtape Letters*, bound with *Screwtape Proposes a Toast*, rev. ed. (New York, N.Y.: Macmillan Publishing Co., 1982), p. 56.

But imagine—just imagine—what would happen if our thoughts focused not on bitterness but on the forgiveness of Christ . . . not on our fears but on the hope we have in Christ . . . not on the selfish accumulation of things but on the unselfishness of the Savior . . . not on exalted thoughts of ourselves but on His lowliness.

May I lift the shade on your personal thoughts and take a peek? What clutters your cranium? Work? Worries? What-might-have-been's?

____

____

____

What shape are they molding you into?

____

____

____

If you don't like the life your thoughts are designing for you, why not rearrange your mental furniture around Jesus? As a prelude to what we'll be learning in the next chapter, memorize Hebrews 12:1–3 and let it guide you in filling those inner spaces of your heart and mind.

> Therefore, since we have so great a cloud of witnesses surrounding us, let us also lay aside every encumbrance, and the sin which so easily entangles us, and let us run with endurance the race that is set before us, fixing our eyes on Jesus, the author and perfecter of faith, who for the joy set before Him endured the cross, despising the shame, and has sat down at the right hand of the throne of God. For consider Him who has endured such hostility by sinners against Himself, so that you may not grow weary and lose heart.

Chapter 2

IT STARTS IN YOUR MIND

(PART TWO)

Selected Scriptures

Mediocrity germinates in the fallen Eden of the mind. Every compromised seed of thought sown or dropped in the brain's gray furrows gestates silently, awaiting a springtime opportunity at new life. There it will sprout to full bloom and reproduce after its kind—yielding labyrinths of thistles and thorns and choking vines that reach into every corner, touch every thought, every feeling, every attitude.

For the mind is not fallow ground but fertile soil. If nurtured, it will bring forth orchards of fruit; if neglected, acres of frustration.

We have in our favor the sharp hoe of the Spirit, which can till the hardest of hearts and uproot the most stubborn of mental weeds. But that hoe must be held with hands that are both vigilant and diligent, because the garden is every inch a war zone, and the gardener must watch as well as work.

So, if we are ever to rise above mediocrity, we must first cultivate our minds. If we don't, they will become brier patches of tangled, destructive thoughts. Instead of becoming captive to Christ, our thoughts will run rampant, choking out anything good that has ever been planted. And Satan will claim the territory by virtue of squatter's rights.

The Schemes of Satan

As we begin a crop-dusting flight over our mental fields, let's take another look at the terrain we plowed in the previous lesson.

> Put on the full armor of God, that you may be able to stand firm against the schemes of the devil. For our struggle is not against flesh and blood, but against the rulers, against the powers, against the world forces of this darkness, against the spiritual forces of wickedness in the heavenly places. (Eph. 6:11–12)

Like an army of invading insects, Satan's ravenous horde is everywhere. His hierarchy ranges from kings to pawns, all dark pieces on the chessboard where he plots his every move with ruthless cunning. And his number one strategy is to keep God's kingdom in check.

> Even if our gospel is veiled, it is veiled to those who are perishing, in whose case the god of this world has blinded the minds of the unbelieving, that they might not see the light of the gospel of the glory of Christ, who is the image of God. (2 Cor. 4:3–4)

What is Satan's scheme? To blind the minds of the lost concerning the truth of the salvation Jesus offers. In order to penetrate that spiritual darkness, the Holy Spirit must lift the scales off their spiritual eyesight. Satan's attacks are aimed primarily at the mind—a fortress under constant assault.

> For though we walk in the flesh, we do not war according to the flesh, for the weapons of our warfare are not of the flesh, but divinely powerful for the destruction of fortresses. We are destroying speculations and every lofty thing raised up against the knowledge of God, and we are taking every thought captive to the obedience of Christ. (10:3–5)

For the carnal individual, the entire mind is a fortress that walls out God. If the Spirit does penetrate such a mind, Satan quickly tries to rebuild those carnal walls, to shore up the towers, and to provide a steady stream of sentries to rebuff the Spirit's offensive. It is the Spirit's job to conquer this carnal mind and bring it into subjection. Once God gains control over that rebel territory, Satan is forced to abdicate his position. But he never gives up easily; instead, he launches a barrage of counteroffensives. And he looks for any crack in the wall to gain an advantage.

The Seeds of Scripture

As every acorn contains a forest of oaks, so every seed of God's truth contains a potential orchard of spiritual fruit. If God's fruit is to triumph over Satan's weeds, His Word must be sown not only far and wide but deep as well. The best way to begin doing that is to plant the Scriptures firmly in your mind, to memorize God's powerful truths.

Planting the Word

Romans 6:12–13 gives us our chores for the day's work ahead of us.

> Therefore do not let sin reign in your mortal body that you should obey its lusts, and do not go on presenting the members of your body to sin as instruments of unrighteousness; but present yourselves to God as those alive from the dead, and your members as instruments of righteousness to God.

Such clear, pure counsel—yet the nagging question is *how*. How do I yield myself to God? David frames a similar question in Psalm 119:9 and immediately provides the answer.

> How can a young man keep his way pure?
> By keeping it according to Thy word.

Still other questions elbow their way through the crowd of theological issues: How can I keep God's Word? Where do I begin? Again, David hands our begging questions a nourishing answer.

> Thy word I have treasured in my heart,
> That I may not sin against Thee. (v. 11)

The harvest of a thousand bushels begins with a seed, and a life of righteousness begins with the right seeds planted early in life. Notice the emphasis in Proverbs on letting the seeds of wisdom our parents planted in our minds take root.

> When I was a son to my father,
> Tender and the only son in the sight of my mother,
> Then he taught me and said to me,
> "Let your heart hold fast my words;
> Keep my commandments and live." . . .
> My son, keep my words,
> And treasure my commandments within you.
> Keep my commandments and live,
> And my teaching as the apple of your eye.
> Bind them on your fingers;
> Write them on the tablet of your heart. . . .
> Incline your ear and hear the words of the wise,
> And apply your mind to my knowledge;
> For it will be pleasant if you keep them within you,

That they may be ready on your lips.
(Prov. 4:3–4; 7:1–3; 22:17–18)

If we are to so treasure the words of our parents, how much more should we treasure the Word of God in our hearts and value it above all other advice!

To many of us, however, memorizing Scripture is like plowing without a mule, let alone a tractor. And that's a pretty tough row to hoe. If that's the case with you, here are some tips to help make it easier.

1. Choose a time and place where you can be free from distractions.
2. Set aside an adequate slice of time to tackle the task, say, fifteen to forty-five minutes.
3. Check the context carefully to make sure the verse should be applied to believers today.
4. Read the text aloud. Read it slowly, over and over, until you can repeat it confidently and without error.
5. Break the passage down into a natural cadence of phrases or thoughts in order to capture its rhythm.
6. Repeat the reference often to help orient yourself to the verse's biblical neighborhood. If you ever get a little turned around, it's always nice to have an address handy to help find your way home.
7. Underline the words or phrases you stumble over to help you walk securely through the passage.
8. Record in a notebook at the end of the day what you have learned from the passage and how the Lord has used it in your life.

Personalizing the Word

Another technique in equipping yourself with God's Word is to personalize His message to you. An effective way to do this is to substitute appropriate personal pronouns into the biblical text, for example: *I*, *me*, *my*, or *mine*. In John 3:16, for instance, you would say "God so loved *me*" instead of "God so loved the world."

Analyzing the Word

Finally, use the passage you've memorized as a magnifying glass to analyze how the Word relates to your life. How does the verse affect your view of God? Of yourself? Your mate? Your children? Your friendships? What changes does the verse challenge you to make?

Harvesting the Word

Planting the Word in your heart, personalizing it, and analyzing it for application will enable you to reap bushels of benefits.

- It will help you gain control of your thought life.
- It will make you more alert to the needs of others and more sensitive to their circumstances.
- It will give your counsel the edge of truth that comes from God rather than limited human wisdom.
- It will sharpen your teaching skills and as a result, your effectiveness and confidence will increase.

Such a bountiful harvest! Won't you begin uprooting the weeds of mediocrity and planting the seeds of God's truth in the fertile soil of your mind today?

Living Insights STUDY ONE

The message of this study is clear: If we expect to be victorious in our thought life, we must memorize God's Word. In our second Living Insight from the previous chapter, we set about learning by heart Hebrews 12:1–3. How did you do? Using the eight guidelines from this chapter, evaluate your method of memorization and note any changes you could make that would be helpful.

1. What time and place did you choose? Were you free from distractions? If not, where else could you go for quiet, undisturbed time?

2. How much time did you set aside? Did it feel like too much? Too little?

3. Were you familiar with the context of this passage? If not, take some time to read through Hebrews 11 and the balance of 12.

4. How did you read the text? Silently and quickly? Or out loud until it felt comfortable? Are you reading from a version that fits naturally with your way of speaking?

5. How did you break the passage down? Did you try to grasp too much all at once? Were you attuned to the rhythm of the phrases?

6. Did you remember to include the "biblical address" as you memorized the passage?

7. What words or phrases did you stumble over, if any? Try underlining or highlighting the places that tripped you up, and see if that will help you walk more securely through the passage.

8. If you don't keep a notebook or journal, use the space provided here to record what you learned from that passage, how God used it in your life, how it touched your heart.

Living Insights STUDY TWO

Satan preys on the mind that is ignorant. He buffets the mind driven by emotion. But nothing fends him off like the Sword of the Spirit.

Where are you in the discipline of Scripture memorization? For some, this chapter has served as an encouraging review. For others, it has been motivation to reestablish a slipping practice. And for still others, the concept of memorization is brand-new. Whichever category you fall into, you'll be sure to benefit from strengthening your Scripture memorization skills.

Two helpful memory systems we recommend come from the ministry of the Navigators. The first is *The Navigators Scripture Memory Course: Topical Memory System;* and the second is their *Life Issues* topical memory system, which deals with issues such as anger, sin, stress, money, and love. Your local Christian bookstore should have information about these.

Chapter 3

It Involves His Kingdom

(PART ONE)

Selected Scriptures

Psalm 103:19 crystallizes the essence of the kingdom of God.

> The Lord has established His throne in the heavens;
> And His sovereignty rules over all.

From Eden's brief innocence to today's permeating corruption, God's kingdom has remained intact. Amazingly, God still offers us His kingdom—even though we rebel against it. He is still eager to pour out righteousness and peace and joy . . . still eager to give power.

The question is, are we willing to accept His power, to submit to His sovereign rule, to live our lives for the furtherance of His kingdom rather than hinder it through settling for mediocrity's status quo?

If living on the heights of God's eternal, unspoilable kingdom appeals to you more than ossifying in the drab flatlands of mediocrity, then let's journey together through Scripture to gain a fuller understanding of what God's kingdom is and how we can be a part of it.

Understanding What the Kingdom Is

The kingdom we're talking about isn't a literal empire but a spiritual reign with unique characteristics and a history all its own.[1]

Kingdom Characteristics

First, *it isn't physical, but it is spiritual.* The apostle Paul tells us that "the kingdom of God is not eating and drinking, but righteousness and peace and joy in the Holy Spirit" (Rom. 14:17). So it's not something we can physically touch or taste. But it is full of the Spirit's fruit to feast on (see Ps. 34:8).

1. The kingdom we're referring to here is not the physical messianic kingdom but "the kingdom of God in the spiritual sense in which it already exists in the souls of believers." Frederic Louis Godet, *Commentary on the First Epistle of St. Paul to the Corinthians*, trans. A. Cusin (1886; reprint, Grand Rapids, Mich.: Zondervan Publishing House, 1957), vol. 1, p. 236. See also Philip E. Hughes, *A Commentary on the Epistle to the Hebrews* (Grand Rapids, Mich.: William B. Eerdmans Publishing Co., 1977), p. 559.

Second, *it isn't audible, but it is powerful.* "For the kingdom of God does not consist in words, but in power," Paul told the Corinthians (1 Cor. 4:20). Like lightning that displays its bright, white strength without a sound, the kingdom of God offers not words, but power.

And third, *it isn't visible, but it is unshakable.* Hebrews 12:28 assures us: "Therefore, since we receive a kingdom which cannot be shaken, let us show gratitude, by which we may offer to God an acceptable service with reverence and awe." This kingdom full of good things—joy, peace, righteousness, power—has God's own everlasting stability to anchor it. In a world of constant change and upheaval, how thankful we can be for something that will remain the same "yesterday and today, yes and forever" (13:8).

The kingdom, then, is the invisible realm where God exercises His full authority over every part of us—over our hearts, our minds, our wills.

Kingdom History

To nutshell the movement of God's kingdom through time, we can use this basic outline.

1. God creates all things and establishes His authority over all (Gen. 1 and 2). From the plant kingdom to the animal kingdom to humanity, God's rule is intended to encompass all the kingdoms of the earth.

2. Humankind rebels against God's authority (Gen. 3). With the enemy's encouragement, our Edenic ancestors yelled defiantly, "I will rule my own life! I will establish my own kingdom."

3. God moves through history to reestablish His authority (Gen. 4–Rev. 22). From the beginning of time, we mortals have fought God for His immortal throne. Still raising arms against His rule, we're in the heat of this battle today (compare Matt. 6:24, 33).

Viewing the Kingdom through an Old Testament Example

One graphic example of this battle for sovereignty is found in the life of the Babylonian king Nebuchadnezzar. Although the word *kingdom* is never mentioned in his story, its message fills the pages of his biography. Nebuchadnezzar is one man who learned the hard way who belongs on the throne of our hearts.

The Dream

One night King Nebuchadnezzar had a troubling dream, and he ordered all the wise men of Babylon to come before him to interpret it. But Daniel, the king's young Hebrew hostage, was the only one who could decode the nightmare. He told King Nebuchadnezzar:

> "'The tree that you saw, which became large and grew strong, whose height reached to the sky and was visible to all the earth, and whose foliage was beautiful and its fruit abundant, and in which was food for all, under which the beasts of the field dwelt and in whose branches the birds of the sky lodged—it is you, O king; for you have become great and grown strong, and your majesty has become great and reached to the sky and your dominion to the end of the earth. And in that the king saw an angelic watcher, a holy one, descending from heaven and saying, "Chop down the tree and destroy it; yet leave the stump with its roots in the ground, but with a band of iron and bronze around it in the new grass of the field, and let him be drenched with the dew of heaven, and let him share with the beasts of the field until seven periods of time pass over him."'" (Dan. 4:20–23)

The Interpretation

Daniel then hit him with the meaning:

> "'This is the interpretation, O king, and this is the decree of the Most High, which has come upon my lord the king: that you be driven away from mankind, and your dwelling place be with the beasts of the field, and you be given grass to eat like cattle and be drenched with the dew of heaven; and seven periods of time will pass over you, until you recognize that the Most High is ruler over the realm of mankind, and bestows it on whomever He wishes. And in that it was commanded to leave the stump with the roots of the tree, your kingdom will be assured to you after you recognize that it is Heaven that rules. Therefore, O king, may my advice be pleasing

> to you: break away now from your sins by doing righteousness, and from your iniquities by showing mercy to the poor, in case there may be a prolonging of your prosperity.'"[2] (vv. 24–27)

The King's Haughty Response

Do you think Nebuchadnezzar heeded Daniel's plea for repentance? Not on your life.

> "Twelve months later he was walking on the roof of the royal palace of Babylon. The king reflected and said, 'Is this not Babylon the great, which *I myself* have built as a royal residence by the might of *my* power and for the glory of *my* majesty?'" (vv. 29–30, emphasis added)

The Fulfillment

Surveying all he had created, King Nebuchadnezzar almost broke his arm patting himself on the back. But look what happened next.

> "While the word was in the king's mouth, a voice came from heaven, saying, 'King Nebuchadnezzar, to you it is declared: sovereignty has been removed from you, and you will be driven away from mankind, and your dwelling place will be with the beasts of the field. You will be given grass to eat like cattle, and seven periods of time will pass over you, until you recognize that the Most High is ruler over the realm of mankind, and bestows it on whomever He wishes.'" (vv. 31–32)

This shuddering decree became reality just seconds after it was made.

> "Immediately the word concerning Nebuchadnezzar

2. "It is interesting to find Daniel advising the king to seek to avert the coming disaster by the practice of meritorious works. . . . It is unfortunate when the Christian doctrine of justification by faith is presented in such a way that the challenge of the moral law is obscured. The problem is to find the right place for morality. . . . Good works are not to be despised. What Christianity supplies is a new motive for performing them." Norman Porteous, *Daniel* (London, England: SCM Press, 1965), pp. 71–72.

> was fulfilled; and he was driven away from mankind and began eating grass like cattle, and his body was drenched with the dew of heaven, until his hair had grown like eagles' feathers and his nails like birds' claws." (v. 33)

The King's Humble Response

Nebuchadnezzar's own sovereignty had been completely removed; his will, broken. A helpless, dew-drenched beast, he finally turned his eyes heavenward.

> "But at the end of that period I, Nebuchadnezzar, raised my eyes toward heaven, and my reason returned to me, and I blessed the Most High and praised and honored Him who lives forever. . . . Now I Nebuchadnezzar praise, exalt, and honor the King of heaven, for all *His* works are true and *His* ways just, and *He* is able to humble those who walk in pride." (vv. 34a, 37; emphasis added)

Notice the change in pronouns? The king no longer gloried in "*my* power" and "*my* majesty" but in "*His* works" and "*His* ways." With his perspective right at last, Nebuchadnezzar was restored and lifted up once again—but this time on the foundation of God's authority (v. 36; compare James 4:10).

Hearing the Kingdom Proclaimed

The biblical mural of God's sovereign authority doesn't stop in the Old Testament—its colors blaze through the New as well. Let's look now at five literary cameos from the book of Acts that will help fill out our understanding of God's kingdom.

Acts 8:10–13

Simon was a magician who had been esteemed in Samaritan eyes as "the Great Power of God" (v. 10). But when Philip the apostle preached "the good news about the kingdom" (v. 12), Simon reached out to God and was saved.

> Even Simon himself believed; and after being baptized, he continued on with Philip; and as he observed signs and great miracles taking place, he was constantly amazed. (v. 13)

The observation is clear: *The message of the kingdom diminishes all other powers*. When confronted with God's power, even Simon—a man with magical power—fell on his face to worship God.

Acts 14:19–22

A few chapters farther on in Acts, we find our next cameo of God's kingdom. Here Paul, still black and blue from an earlier stoning in Lystra, returned to that same city to bring his kingdom message.

> But the Jews came from Antioch and Iconium, and having won over the multitudes, they stoned Paul and dragged him out of the city, supposing him to be dead. But while the disciples stood around him, he arose and entered the city. And the next day he went away with Barnabas to Derbe. And after they had preached the gospel to that city and had made many disciples, they returned to Lystra and to Iconium and to Antioch, strengthening the souls of the disciples, encouraging them to continue in the faith, and saying, "Through many tribulations we must enter the kingdom of God." (vv. 19–22)

Paul's message is certain: *Kingdom living includes many tribulations.*

Acts 19:8–9

Later, in Ephesus—the cosmopolitan kingdom of international commerce—Paul spent three months in the synagogue "reasoning and persuading them about the kingdom of God" (19:8b). When some of the Ephesian Jews, however, became "hardened and disobedient, speaking evil of the Way before the multitude" (v. 9), Paul gathered up his little pocket of disciples and withdrew to the school of Tyrannus, where others sat under his instruction for two years.

This New Testament vignette yields another observation: *Kingdom emphasis thins the ranks*. It separates the superficial onlookers from the dedicated disciples.

Acts 20:22–27

In this next scene, Paul was determined to leave his friends at Miletus en route to Jerusalem, knowing that only bondage and affliction awaited him. In verse 24a, he explained the reason for his fortitude:

> "But I do not consider my life of any account as dear to myself."

Only a person with kingdom perspective could say this and remain honest. Paul went on to further unravel the meaning of the kingdom.

> "And now, behold, I know that all of you, among whom I went about preaching *the kingdom*, will see my face no more. Therefore I testify to you this day, that I am innocent of the blood of all men. For I did not shrink from declaring to you *the whole purpose of God*." (vv. 25–27, emphasis added)

In this monologue, Paul linked God's kingdom with God's purpose. The observation stands boldly: *The kingdom is central to the whole purpose of God.*

Acts 28:23

Here Paul was under house arrest in Rome, talking to a crowd of people who had come to see him. Notice what he chose to tell them.

> He was explaining to them by solemnly testifying about the kingdom of God, and trying to persuade them concerning Jesus, from both the Law of Moses and from the Prophets, from morning until evening. (v. 23b)

Notice, too, that the same two messages stayed on his heart during his entire imprisonment.

> And he stayed two full years in his own rented quarters, and was welcoming all who came to him, preaching the kingdom of God, and teaching concerning the Lord Jesus Christ with all openness, unhindered. (vv. 30–31)

These passages provide a final observation: *The kingdom is inseparably linked to the Lord Jesus Christ.* All conversation about the kingdom, however unobtrusive, invariably winds its way to the lordship of Christ. And the signposts along the way tell us to give up all we have in order to accept all He has to give us.

A Parting Word

We squirm inside whenever we're asked to throw ourselves completely into any one thing—sometimes rightly so. In the case of the father who's asked to sacrifice everything for his company . . . the athlete who's required to give up everything for the team . . . the doctor who's called on to abandon everything for the practice, overcommitment often needs to be wrestled to the ground.

But when it comes to the kingdom commitment of surrendering our hearts to God, we're best off holding nothing back. We can never obey God too fully—never love Jesus too deeply—never relinquish too much. Never.

Living Insights STUDY ONE

As we learned in this chapter, the kingdom is the invisible realm where God exercises His full authority over every part of our lives—including our hearts, our minds, and our wills. It's not so much an external, physical place as it is an inner, spiritual realm. God's kingdom is a kingdom of souls; its borders are expanded one person at a time.

Our lives, then, are to reflect the glory of God's kingdom to others, to stand above mediocrity's stagnation and beacon others to life in Christ's saving light. But how on earth can people like us accomplish such a task? Are there any specifics to living as citizens of God's kingdom? Is there anything else about the kingdom we should be aware of?

Graciously, God has given us high ideals to reach for and clear pictures of what His marvelous kingdom is like. We've already looked at several of these from Scripture, but let's take time to gaze at some more. In the space provided, jot down the wonders you find in each of the following passages; then note the ways this aspect of kingdom citizenship can shine in your life.

Psalm 45:1–4a, 6–7a ______________________________

____

____

Isaiah 9:6–7 ____________________________________

Daniel 7:27 ______________________________

____

____

Matthew 5:3, 10 ______________________________

____

____

Matthew 18:3–4 ______________________________

____

____

Romans 14:17 ______________________________

____

____

1 Corinthians 6:9–11 ______________________________

____

____

Colossians 1:13–14 ______________________________

____

____

James 2:5 ______________________________

____

____

Revelation 1:6 ______________________________

Living Insights STUDY TWO

We all long for the day when Christ's kingdom of righteousness and peace and joy is realized fully on this earth. What often surprises us, however, is the fact that kingdom living in the meantime includes many tribulations. This takes us off guard, and we easily lose our bearings as we wonder what went wrong. But F. B. Meyer shows us that when things seem amiss, they are actually going *right*.

> If in an unknown country, I am informed that I must pass through a valley where the sun is hidden, or over a stony bit of road, to reach my abiding place—when I come to it, each moment of shadow or jolt of the carriage tells me that I am on the right road.[3]

"The right road"! Have you ever thought of those bumps and bruises and shadows and jolts of your life as a confirming sign that you're on the right road?

There really is no easy street when we're following Christ, and the toll along the way is often suffering (Phil. 1:29; 3:10; 1 Pet. 2:21; 4:19). But we can take comfort in where that road of suffering leads—to our being conformed to the image of the ever-living Christ (Rom. 8:29). As George Macdonald reminds us:

> The Son of God suffered unto the death, not that men might not suffer, but that their sufferings might be like His.[4]

3. F. B. Meyer, *Christ in Isaiah* (Fort Washington, Pa.: Christian Literature Crusade, n.d.), p. 9.

4. George Macdonald, as quoted by C. S. Lewis in *The Problem of Pain* (New York, N.Y.: Collier Books, Macmillan Publishing Co., 1962), epigraph.

Chapter 4

IT INVOLVES HIS KINGDOM
(PART TWO)

Selected Scriptures

Each decade, like a feature film headed for the big screen, is incomplete without its actors, setting, props, costumes, and musical score. Together, these express the tone of the times.

The sixties. The actors, "hippies," wore as little as possible, and what they did wear was tattered and tie-dyed. Passion burned like incense in the communal air. Amplified by Bob Dylan, Simon and Garfunkel, and the Beatles, their psychedelic feelings of love and peace and freedom expressed themselves everywhere—in their music, their art, even on bathroom walls. They were committed to reaching out to others, getting involved in social causes, and rebelling hard against anything that threatened their utopian ideals. Their thinking was centrifugal—outward and other-oriented.

The eighties. The "yuppies"—young, upwardly mobile professionals—starred in that decade. This era reeked with a dress-for-success, look-out-for-number-one attitude. The props were sushi and Perrier, BMWs and tanning oils. Their score was synthesized jazz on compact discs, piped through high-tech stereo systems. Committed to their own success, these power seekers climbed the corporate ladder hand over hand, rung for rung, knocking away anything or anyone that threatened to hinder their ascent. Yuppie thinking was centripetal—like a draining hot tub whose water is sucked into the center.

The cultural aura of our times inevitably seeps in to poison our thinking; we cannot live completely unaffected by it. Fortunately, though, living in God's spiritual kingdom cannot help but affect and change us too—only for the better. In this chapter we will see how kingdom living is sure to dilute our baneful philosophies and purify the turbid tributaries of our minds.

A Few Reminders

Before building on the foundation of the last lesson, let's retighten our grip on a few of the kingdom's nuts and bolts.

The Meaning of the Kingdom

In John 3, Jesus explains to Nicodemus that we must enter the kingdom by a new birth . . . that we will never experience it through the warmth of the womb.

> Jesus answered and said to him, "Truly, truly, I say to you, unless one is born again, he cannot see the kingdom of God." Nicodemus said to Him, "How can a man be born when he is old? He cannot enter a second time into his mother's womb and be born, can he?" Jesus answered, "Truly, truly, I say to you, unless one is born of water and the Spirit, he cannot enter into the kingdom of God." (vv. 3–5)

Just what is this kingdom? It's God's authority over our lives. It's His supreme right to rule. It's letting Him call the shots, unbegrudgingly. We enter the kingdom by a new birth, and we thrive in it by a constant pursuit of righteousness.

> "But seek first His kingdom and His righteousness; and all these things shall be added to you." (Matt. 6:33; see also 5:6; Luke 1:74–75)

How different from the "me-first" message of the yuppies—or even the "others-first" cry of the hippies. In God's kingdom, God is first.

Our Struggle with the Kingdom

Luke 19 tells two stories that depict both sides of the struggle to let God be first. One shows a man released from the clutches of his own will by the accepting words of Jesus (v. 5); the other shows a group of slaves who chose to resist the tug of the kingdom.

The first story is a true one. It's about Zaccheus—a corrupt tax collector infatuated with riches, who decided to relinquish his selfish striving and follow Christ. Listen to his words of repentance:

> "Behold, Lord, half of my possessions I will give to the poor, and if I have defrauded anyone of anything, I will give back four times as much." (v. 8)

Jesus' grace-filled response to him also revealed His mission:

> "Today salvation has come to this house, . . . for the Son of Man has come to seek and to save that

which was lost." (vv. 9–10)

Notice, Jesus did not come to dazzle us with His power nor to manipulate people or make Himself a name. He didn't come to manufacture success. He came to seek and to save the lost. He came to give up His rights so that the Father's will would be done (see 22:42).

The second story, a parable, illustrates the flip side of our struggle—our resistance to the kingdom.

> "A certain nobleman went to a distant country to receive a kingdom for himself, and then return. And he called ten of his slaves, and gave them ten minas, and said to them, 'Do business with this until I come back.' But his citizens hated him, and sent a delegation after him, saying, *'We do not want this man to reign over us.'*" (19:12–14, emphasis added)

This is the response many give today when asked to live under the lordship of Christ. We've worked hard to earn our degrees, carve out our careers, secure our positions and perks. So we figure we've earned the right to call our own shots and live life the way we please.

Remember, however, that like the citizens in the parable, Zaccheus also wrestled with the kingdom. And though it was Jesus who won the match, it was really Zaccheus who took home the trophy.

Are you saved, but still struggling on the mat, sweating and grunting, trying to avert Jesus' authority with quick, cunning moves? As long as you refuse to forfeit the match against the kingdom, your trophy will be an inner thirst that no success or status can ever quench.

Some Important Applications

How can we strengthen our desire to accept God's right to rule? Let's take a closer look at the snapshots we glanced at in the previous chapter and gather some personal applications—applications that may make us squirm a little but will lead us to new kingdom heights.

Acts 8:10–24

The story of Simon the magician, the man known as the Great Power of God, shows us how to approach—and *not* approach—the kingdom of God. Let's consider the lesson he learned.

> But when they believed Philip preaching the good news about the kingdom of God and the name of Jesus Christ, they were being baptized, men and women alike. And even Simon himself believed; and after being baptized, he continued on with Philip; and as he observed signs and great miracles taking place, he was constantly amazed. (vv. 12–13)

Hearing that the Samaritans had received God's Word, the apostles in Jerusalem sent Peter and John to them to pray "that they might receive the Holy Spirit" (v. 15). So

> they began laying their hands on them, and they were receiving the Holy Spirit. (v. 17)

Simon was so arrested by their miraculous works that he, too, wanted a piece of the pie.

> Now when Simon saw that the Spirit was bestowed through the laying on of the apostles' hands, he offered them money, saying, "Give this authority to me as well, so that everyone on whom I lay my hands may receive the Holy Spirit." (vv. 18–19)

But Peter's words of rebuke grabbed Simon by the nape of the neck:

> "May your silver perish with you, because you thought you could obtain the gift of God with money! You have no part or portion in this matter, for your heart is not right before God. Therefore repent of this wickedness of yours, and pray the Lord that if possible, the intention of your heart may be forgiven you. For I see that you are in the gall of bitterness and in the bondage of iniquity." (vv. 20–23)

Like a scolded puppy, Simon whimpered a tail-between-the-legs response.

> Simon answered and said, "Pray to the Lord for me yourselves, so that nothing of what you have said may come upon me." (v. 24)

From Simon's humbling experience this application can be drawn: *When facing the temptation to make a name, call on kingdom power*. Sometimes our gifts pave a way for us to become popular and powerful, and we can be tempted to get puffed up and strut around demanding special treatment. That's when we need to remember the kingdom's emphasis on the importance of small, quiet things rather than loud, flashy feats. As Richard Foster observes:

> In experiences of hiddenness we learn that the ministry of small things is a necessary prerequisite to the ministry of power. . . .
>
> Small things are the genuinely big things in the kingdom of God. It is here we truly face the issues of obedience and discipleship. It is not hard to be a model disciple amid camera lights and press releases. But in the small corners of life, in those areas of service that will never be newsworthy or gain us any recognition, we must hammer out the meaning of obedience. Amid the obscurity of family and friends, neighbors and work associates, we find God.[1]

Acts 14:21–22

Moving from Samaria to Lystra, we find another challenging application. After his stoning in Lystra, remember, Paul brushed himself off, traveled to Derbe to proclaim the gospel message, and then returned to the very place where he had been stoned! Once there he strengthened

> the souls of the disciples, encouraging them to continue in the faith, and saying, "Through many tribulations we must enter the kingdom of God." (v. 22)

The message on Paul's heart was suffering—a message loathed by every person who wants an easy road and instant gratification. But to be part of the kingdom is to suffer: "And indeed, all who desire to live godly in Christ Jesus will be persecuted" (2 Tim. 3:12; see also Phil. 1:29; 1 Pet. 3:14). The application? *When going through times of testing, count on kingdom endurance*. Another page from the journal of Paul's heart reveals how the kingdom kept him enduring through suffering.

1. Richard J. Foster, *Money, Sex and Power: The Challenge of the Disciplined Life* (San Francisco, Calif.: Harper and Row, Publishers, 1985), pp. 218–19.

> For this reason I endure all things for the sake of those who are chosen, that they also may obtain the salvation which is in Christ Jesus and with it eternal glory. It is a trustworthy statement:
>
> For if we died with Him, we shall also live
> with Him;
> If we endure, we shall also reign with Him.
> (2 Tim. 2:10–12a)

Knowing that we have a part in bringing others to eternal life and that Christ has privileged us with reigning next to Him can keep us going in times of strain and sorrow.

Acts 19:8–9

In Ephesus, Paul brought his kingdom message into the synagogue.

> And he entered the synagogue and continued speaking out boldly for three months, reasoning and persuading them about the kingdom of God. (v. 8)

Speaking, reasoning, persuading.[2] Why the strong verbs to describe Paul's ministry to the Ephesians? Because they were not easily touched by talk about the kingdom. Their hearts were hardened—calloused and cold.

> But when some were becoming hardened[3] and disobedient, speaking evil of the Way before the multitude, he withdrew from them and took away the disciples, reasoning daily in the school of Tyrannus. (v. 9)

Because of the hard-heartedness of some of the Ephesians, Paul withdrew to teach his disciples in the school of Tyrannus. There's an important application to be made from this account: *When wondering why some walk away, realize that the kingdom separates.*

2. *Speaking* means "to declare as if making a proclamation." *Reasoning* means "dialoguing," which includes the ideas of "pondering" and "debating." And *persuading* means "to prevail upon so as to bring about a change."

3. *Hardened* means "dry" and conveys the idea of being austere and stern and severe.

Acts 20:17–27

Here we see Paul in the little town of Miletus, bidding tearful good-byes to the elders of the church at Ephesus. He said to them,

> "And now, behold, I know that all of you, among whom I went about preaching the kingdom, will see my face no more. Therefore I testify to you this day, that I am innocent of the blood of all men. For I did not shrink from declaring to you the whole purpose of God." (vv. 25–27)

In our generation, it's easy to shrink from the kingdom message, for it requires long-term commitment and self-sacrifice.

> For the time will come when they will not endure sound doctrine; but wanting to have their ears tickled, they will accumulate for themselves teachers in accordance to their own desires. (2 Tim. 4:3)

But kingdom living—the message that cuts so deeply into the lives of those who hear it—lies at the core of God's purpose. The application is clear: *When coming to terms with the whole purpose of God, remember kingdom commitment.*

Acts 28:23–24, 30–31

We next find Paul sharing his faith with people who were anxious to hear about it.

> And he was explaining to them by solemnly testifying about the kingdom of God, and trying to persuade them concerning Jesus. (v. 23b)

Verses 30–31 show the content of Paul's message:

> And he stayed two full years in his own rented quarters, and was welcoming all who came to him, preaching the kingdom of God, and teaching concerning the Lord Jesus Christ with all openness, unhindered.

The kingdom and the Lord Jesus Christ are two inseparable links in the chain of faith. The application: *When sharing your faith, include kingdom authority.*

A Concluding Application

Like the hippies of the sixties and the yuppies of the eighties, cast members of God's kingdom all read the same script. The set combines heavenly principles with earthly realities. The props are the fruits of righteousness and peace and joy (Rom. 14:17). The cast may be costumed in frayed cutoffs or tweed blazers, but all of them are clothed in the righteousness of Jesus.

The kingdom requires neither the idealistic rebellion of the sixties nor the casual self-absorption of the eighties. It asks for a surrendered will, an acknowledgment of God's authority over every area of our lives.

Is the theme song of your life "Have Thine Own Way, Lord"? Is His purpose your purpose; His will, your will? If not, Jesus is waiting for you to descend your heart's throne and let Him be king . . . and make the glories of His kingdom a reality in your life.

> "The kingdom of heaven is like a treasure hidden in the field, which a man found and hid; and from joy over it he goes and sells all that he has, and buys that field." (Matt. 13:44)[4]

Living Insights — STUDY ONE

If we seriously desire to follow Christ, we must allow kingdom teachings to penetrate our personal lives. In the space provided, write how you can personalize each of the five applications from this chapter. Begin by asking yourself, What difference can this principle make in my life?

When facing the temptation to make a name, call on kingdom power.

4. For a poignant description of the kingdom, see John White's book *Magnificent Obsession*, rev. ed. (Downers Grove, Ill.: InterVarsity Press, 1990), pp. 30–33. This book was formerly titled *The Cost of Commitment*.

When going through times of testing, count on kingdom endurance.

When wondering why some walk away, realize that the kingdom separates.

When coming to terms with the whole purpose of God, remember kingdom commitment.

When sharing your faith, include kingdom authority.

Living Insights

STUDY TWO

What does it take to experience God's kingdom? In brief, it takes giving the King full authority over every part of your life. Easy to say—harder to live out.

There's a tremendously important issue at stake here. It's well worth your time to think through an answer. How can kingdom living help you live above the level of mediocrity? Write your thoughts in the space provided, and be as specific as you can.

Chapter 5

It Costs Your Commitment

Luke 14:25–33

Great leaders are those who clearly state the cost of the commitment their followers must make—no matter how demanding or dangerous that commitment might be.

King Arthur was such a leader. His knights came to him with zeal and enthusiasm, but he bound them to himself with vows that required the highest level of devotion.

> "Arthur sat
> Crown'd on the daïs, and his warriors cried,
> 'Be thou the king, and we will work thy will
> Who love thee.' Then the King in low deep tones,
> And simple words of great authority,
> Bound them by so strait vows to his own self,
> That when they rose, knighted from kneeling, some
> Were pale as at the passing of a ghost,
> Some flush'd, and others dazed, as one who wakes
> Half-blinded at the coming of a light."[1]

No leader requires such "strait vows" of loyalty as Jesus. If we are to follow Him, we will have to count the cost . . . and the cost is as exacting now as it was when Jesus walked the earth. Let's listen to His words to learn what the cost of commitment to Him entails and see how living consecrated to Christ precludes settling for a half-hearted life of mediocrity.

The Setting

Jesus never sought to attract great crowds, but multitudes just seemed to flock wherever He went. And the standing-room-only audience in Luke 14 was no exception. Some were drawn to His simple stories and clear teaching about spiritual things; others came

1. Allan Knee, ed., *Idylls of the King* and *Camelot* (New York, N.Y.: Dell Publishing Co., 1967), p. 25.

in hopes of being healed. Still others came out of curiosity, craning their necks to see some miracle. Patriots also came—those who, under the restive dominion of Rome, were eager to find a young revolutionary they might recruit as a spokesman for their cause.

The Terms of Consecration

Looking over the sea of faces that followed Him, Jesus—like King Arthur—explicitly states the terms of consecration that He requires of His disciples (Luke 14:26–27, 33).

Personal Relationships

The first and most stringent of the terms is found in verse 26.

> "If anyone comes to Me, and does not hate his own father and mother and wife and children and brothers and sisters, yes, and even his own life, he cannot be My disciple."

No one can ever accuse Christ of beating around the bush or hedging on tough issues. No election-year politics here. Just the truth, unsheathed and unblunted. But *hate?* Such a staggering word. Yet that is His intention—to stagger the crowds, to thin the uncommitted from the ranks. In dramatic fashion, Jesus states the primary condition for discipleship: In the realm of relationships, *He must come first.* Commentator Norval Geldenhuys fleshes out this stark command.

> He who wishes to follow Him must choose Him so unconditionally as Lord and Guide that he makes all other loyalties and ties absolutely subordinate to his loyalty and devotion to Him. The Saviour, of course, does not mean that he who desires to follow Him must hate his parents and other loved ones as such, but certainly that if loyalty to Him clashes with loyalty to them he is to treat his loved ones in this connection *as though* they are persons whom he hates.[2]

2. Norval Geldenhuys, *Commentary on the Gospel of Luke* (Grand Rapids, Mich.: William B. Eerdmans Publishing Co., 1972), p. 398. See also Deuteronomy 13:6–10 for an example of how a clash in loyalties between family and God was to be handled under the old covenant.

Jesus asks for nothing less than our hearts—which cannot be given in halves (see Matt. 6:24; 10:37). All relationships, no matter how intimate, must be secondary to our relationship with Christ. As John White explains,

> To hate one's family means to be so committed to Christ that, however much it costs me to be away from that circle, I must cut myself ruthlessly from its comfort and follow him barefoot on rocky pathways.[3]

Personal Desires

Expanding on the words "even his own life" in Luke 14:26, Jesus tells His followers that to be His disciples they must be willing to sacrifice even the most personal of desires.

> "Whoever does not carry his own cross and come after Me cannot be My disciple." (v. 27)

As these Roman-ruled Palestinians hear His words, they must picture the all-too-familiar scene of criminals trudging to their execution, carrying on their shoulders the very crosses on which they were to suffer. Jesus confronts His listeners with the reality that following Him could cost them their lives—literally. And He offers no padding to cushion their shoulders from the splinters of that cross and no anesthesia for the nails.

In Romans 12:1, Paul employs a similar metaphor to paint with bold strokes the black-and-white realities of discipleship.

> I urge you therefore, brethren, by the mercies of God, to present your bodies a living and holy sacrifice, acceptable to God, which is your spiritual service of worship.

Carrying our cross means charting a path that, every step of the way, leads to death—death to selfishness and self-centeredness. If we want to commit our lives to Christ as His disciples, we have to say no to our self-will, our self-determined goals, our selfish desires. All of these, bound up in our old nature, must be nailed to a cross.

This death, though, is not an end in itself. Paul tells us that Christ died so that we "who live should no longer live for [our]selves" but should live in such a way as "to be pleasing to Him"

3. John White, *Magnificent Obsession*, rev. ed. (Downers Grove, Ill.: InterVarsity Press, 1990), p. 58.

(2 Cor. 5:15a, 9b). And this new ambition, in turn, will change our relationships with those around us:

> Now we who are strong ought to bear the weaknesses of those without strength and not just please ourselves. Let each of us please his neighbor for his good, to his edification. For even Christ did not please Himself. (Rom. 15:1–3a)

Personal Possessions

The third stipulation Jesus insists upon for His followers is a loose grip on all earthly possessions.

> "So therefore, no one of you can be My disciple who does not give up all his own possessions." (Luke 14:33)

If the hand on your possessions is clenched tight, Jesus will not be able to take that hand and lead you very far. At some point, clinging to possessions will pull you away from Christ. Whether a nice house, a new car, or an Ivy League education, if held too tightly possessions will hold you back from fully following Christ.

Is there something in your life that you can't seem to let go of? Do you want it so badly that you don't really possess it anymore, but it possesses you? If the Lord ever chooses to take it, the loss will be a lot less painful if you relax your grip.

The Reasons for Consecration

Christ's disciples are to have Him as their foremost love and have themselves and their possessions in proper perspective behind Him. But why does He state the terms of consecration with such exactness? The reason is found in two penetrating parables.

The Parable of the Improvident Builder

In verses 28–30, Jesus brings His point home with an illustration each listener could relate to.

> "For which one of you, when he wants to build a tower, does not first sit down and calculate the cost, to see if he has enough to complete it? Otherwise, when he has laid a foundation, and is not able to finish, all who observe it begin to ridicule him, saying, 'This man began to build and was not able to finish.'"

Back in those days, the Herods had a passion for erecting elaborate works of architecture. Doubtless, many whose resources were more limited tried to imitate them and ended up with their bank accounts depleted and their buildings unfinished. Pilate, for instance, had begun building an aqueduct which, for lack of funds, was left incomplete. Here Jesus gives the example of a tower that begins as a challenge to the sky and ends up the unsightly stubble of an improvident venture, a mere target for ridicule.

How about you? If the blueprint is the Sermon on the Mount and the cost is everything you hold dear, are you willing to build a life that will stand as a towering testimony for Jesus?

The Parable of the Unprepared King

In a similar illustration found in verses 31–32, Jesus reemphasizes His point.

> "Or what king, when he sets out to meet another king in battle, will not first sit down and take counsel whether he is strong enough with ten thousand men to encounter the one coming against him with twenty thousand? Or else, while the other is still far away, he sends a delegation and asks terms of peace."

The message of the parable is clear: Do not undertake what you have neither the strength nor the will nor the resources to accomplish. The war of the Christian is fought on many fronts—with the outer world, our inner selves, and even the Devil himself. The battle is ruthless. The bullets are real. And the commitment of the soldier determines whether victory or surrender will be the final outcome.

On October 8, 1940, Sir Winston Churchill addressed the House of Commons regarding the war with Hitler. In sobering words similar to Christ's, he prepared his followers for the battle:

> Death and sorrow will be the companions of our journey; hardship our garment; constancy and valor our only shield.[4]

In wartime, soldiers must forego many of the privileges, pleasures, and possessions of the common people. Not because these

4. Winston Churchill, as quoted in *Bartlett's Familiar Quotations*, 15th ed., rev. and enl., ed. Emily Morison Beck (Boston, Mass.: Little, Brown and Co., 1980), p. 744.

things are wrong, but because the more pressing priorities of the war demand their sacrifice. That's Christ's point in this parable.

The Summary

In verses 34–35, Jesus crystallizes His teaching with a metaphor.

> "Therefore, salt is good; but if even salt has become tasteless, with what will it be seasoned? It is useless either for the soil or for the manure pile; it is thrown out. He who has ears to hear, let him hear."

Salt is valuable only when it possesses that special, unique quality of saltiness. Similarly, followers of Jesus are only of practical value when they possess that particular characteristic of Christlikeness.[5]

Our consecration, our commitment, to Christ does indeed involve "strait vows." But He above all others is worthy to be told, "Be *Thou* the King, and we will work *Thy* will who love *Thee*." Will you?

Living Insights STUDY ONE

Soaring above mediocrity takes commitment to Christ; it takes consecrating, devoting, ourselves to Him above all others. This sounds grand and lofty and true—something we'd gladly hand over our hearts to . . . until we look into the tender eyes of our unbelieving fiancé, cradle the baby we've waited so many barren years to have, splash in the bubbling laughter of our unsaved friends, share a secret with that parent we'd do anything for.

No, consecration doesn't come easily.

Are any of your relationships hindering your relationship with Christ? Which one or ones?

How is this relationship keeping you from being completely

5. The character qualities of Christlikeness are pictured in the mosaic commonly referred to as the Beatitudes, found in Matthew 5:1–11. Compare this with verse 13.

devoted to Jesus and following the path of excellence that honors Him?

What do you need to do to reestablish your commitment to Christ?

Tough question, isn't it? It doesn't necessarily mean having to break off a relationship; perhaps it just means standing up for what you profess to believe and not compromising so much, or refocusing your priorities. I don't know. But I do know that Jesus is so willing to help you find the answer because He loves you deeply and has your best at heart. Set aside some time right now to talk with Him about this question. And ask Him for the strength to not settle for mediocrity when you discover the answer.

Living Insights STUDY TWO

> "Whoever does not carry his own cross and come after Me cannot be My disciple." (Luke 14:27)

Have you taken that painful walk to Calvary with your goals and desires and dreams? Have you honestly and objectively taken them before the Lord for His approval? Do they feed your ego more than they honor Him? Are you willing to change them if God shows you that you should?

It is an agonizing task to play the executioner on your life's ambitions—to pound the nails and lift the cross. But just remember: after crucifixion comes resurrection. And out of a cold tomb, God will raise goals and desires warm with new life and power.

> Delight yourself in the Lord;
> And He will give you the desires of your heart.
> (Ps. 37:4)

Chapter 6

It Calls for Extravagant Love

Mark 14:1–9

Many years ago, a tourist group made its way through the house where the great composer Ludwig van Beethoven spent his last years. Reaching his conservatory, the guide paused and whispered reverently, "And here is the master's instrument."

One of the tourists pushed her way to the piano, sat down at the bench, and began to play one of Beethoven's sonatas. "I suppose a lot of people love to play this piano," she remarked.

The guide placed his hand on hers, stilling her music. "Well, when Ignacy Paderewski was here last summer, he was asked by several people to play. But he responded, 'Oh, no! I am not worthy to play the same keyboard as the great Beethoven.'"

Similarly, some scenes in Scripture seem too sacred to touch. Some are majestic psalms of praise; others, like the one we'll view today, are sublime moments of simple devotion.

So, with a reverent hush, let's tiptoe back in time. We'll visit the house where Jesus spent one of His last days, and we'll eavesdrop on a moment of pure, extravagant love.

Setting the Scene

The backdrop to this expression of extravagant love juxtaposes tradition with treachery, religious observance with ruthless opposition.

The Time

Our travel takes us to Jerusalem during the Passover celebration just before Christ's crucifixion.

> Now the Passover and Unleavened Bread was two days off. . . . (Mark 14:1a)

What the Fourth of July is to America, Passover was to ancient Israel, only more so. It was a time of celebrating heartily, of singing great Jewish songs, of reenacting the drama of Israel's deliverance from Egypt. Jews from all over made the pilgrimage to Jerusalem each year to celebrate this pinnacle of religious holidays.

The Atmosphere

At this particular Passover, however, the mood of some is not so festive. Instead of celebrating, a few influential religious leaders are planning an execution.

> The chief priests and the scribes were seeking how to seize Him by stealth, and kill Him; for they were saying, "Not during the festival, lest there be a riot of the people." (vv. 1b–2)[1]

The atmosphere is tense, and the situation delicate, for, as John notes, "many of the Jews were . . . believing in Jesus" (John 12:11). If the plan isn't smoothly and surreptitiously carried out, it could blow up in their faces.

The Place

Having told us of all the turmoil brewing in Jerusalem, Mark shifts scenes and we find ourselves transported a few miles east to a modest home in Bethany.

> And while He was in Bethany at the home of Simon the leper, and reclining at the table . . . (Mark 14:3a)

The home of Simon, the leper whom Jesus had cleansed, serves as one of the final respites for the Savior before He will at last rest His head on the splintered roughness of the cross.

The People

John's gospel fills in a few of the story's more personal details by listing Simon's dinner guests for us. He has invited not only Lazarus, whom Jesus recently raised from the dead, but also Lazarus' sisters, Martha and Mary, along with Judas Iscariot and probably several, if not all, of the other disciples (John 12:1–11).

Devotion and Reaction

Into this serene setting a woman silently enters, and it is she who shows the Savior an extravagant display of love.

1. The word *stealth* in verse 1 means "a trick or surprise attack."

The Woman

> There came a woman with an alabaster vial of very costly perfume of pure nard;[2] and she broke the vial and poured it over His head. (Mark 14:3b)

The woman, John tells us, is Mary (John 12:3).[3] He also adds that she uses her hair to wipe His feet with the perfume.

The Observers

The magnificence of this lavish display of love is marred by the murmur of some money-minded men.

> But some were indignantly remarking to one another, "Why has this perfume been wasted? For this perfume might have been sold for over three hundred denarii,[4] and the money given to the poor." And they were scolding her. (Mark 14:4–5)

On their calculating, utilitarian scale of mediocrity, extravagant devotion held little weight.

The Lord

Jesus intervened not only to stop the scolding but also to give special attention to Mary's devotion.

> But Jesus said, "Let her alone; why do you bother her? She has done a good deed to Me. For the poor you always have with you, and whenever you wish, you can do them good; but you do not always have Me. She has done what she could; she has anointed My body beforehand for the burial." (vv. 6–8)

Death is the last subject anyone would want discussed at a dinner party—talk about quenching a festive mood! But Mary had taken to heart Jesus' words about His imminent death (see

2. Genuine nard was made from dried leaves of a rare and unique Himalayan plant. The particular vase she used, if it was like others used in that day to hold expensive ointment, was itself a thing of beauty and held twelve ounces—a Roman pound (compare John 12:3).

3. Each of the three times we see Mary in the Bible, she is at the feet of Christ (Luke 10:39; John 11:32; 12:3).

4. A denarius was equivalent to a day's wage. Therefore, the perfume would have been worth almost a year's salary.

10:32–34; 12:1–12). She didn't suppress the subject; she faced it—and it grieved her to the point of tears. Jesus saw her act of mourning as an early embalming.

Doubtless, the fragrance drenched His garment and lingered in the fabric, reminding Him subtly—even in the midst of betrayal, desertion, denial, trials, beatings, mockings, and death—that there were those who loved Him. Purely. Deeply. And extravagantly.

A Lasting Memorial

According to John 12:3, the fragrance filled the room. And Jesus said that this aromatic moment, so pleasing to God, would linger through time as a subtly fragrant reminder of this woman's love.

> "And truly I say to you, wherever the gospel is preached in the whole world, that also which this woman has done shall be spoken of in memory of her." (Mark 14:9)

> But thanks be to God, who . . . manifests through us the sweet aroma of the knowledge of Him in every place. For we are a fragrance of Christ to God among those who are being saved and among those who are perishing. (2 Cor. 2:14–15)

Living Insights — STUDY ONE

How pure, how deep, how extravagant is your love for Christ?

If it were your bottle of perfume—a bottle that cost you a year's salary—would you have emptied it on the Savior? Or would you have sold it and given the money to the poor? Or kept it for yourself? Or would you have divided it—maybe 10 percent for the Lord, a percentage for the poor, and the remainder for yourself?

To be sure, there is a time for prudence. But there is also a time for extravagance. There is a time to sell perfume for the poor. But there is also a time to shower it on the Lord.

Living Insights STUDY TWO

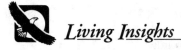

Before you close the door on this chapter, take a deep breath and smell the aroma of extravagant love.

Broken Vases

The aroma of extravagant love.
So pure. So lovely.
Flowing from the veined alabaster vase
  of Mary's broken heart—
A heart broken against the hard reality
  of her Savior's imminent death.
Mingled with tears, the perfume became—
  by some mysterious chemistry of Heaven—
Not diluted, but more concentrated,
Potent enough behind the ears of each century
  for the scent to linger to this day.

Doubtless, the fragrance, absorbed by His garment,
  as it flowed from His head
Accompanied Christ through the humiliation of His trials,
  the indignity of His mockings,
  the pain of His beatings,
  the inhumanity of His cross.
Through the heavy smell of sweat and blood,
A hint of that fragrance must have arisen
  from His garment—
Until, at shameful last, the garment was stripped
  and gambled away.
And maybe, just maybe, it was *that* scent
  amid the stench of humanity rabbled around the cross,
  that gave the Savior the strength to say:
"Father, forgive them, for they know not what they do."

And as Mary walked away from the cross,
The same scent probably still lingered in the now-limp hair
  she used to dry her Savior's feet—
A reminder of the love that spilled
  from His broken alabaster body.

So pure. So lovely.
So *truly* extravagant.

It was a vase He never regretted breaking.
Nor did she.

—Ken Gire

Part Two

Overcoming Mediocrity Means Living Differently

Chapter 7

VISION: SEEING BEYOND THE MAJORITY

Matthew 6:19–34; Numbers 13:1–14:10

In his Harvard commencement address of June 8, 1978, Aleksandr Solzhenitsyn, like a prophet crying in the wilderness, spoke against our tendency to timidly go along with the majority:

> A decline in courage may be the most striking feature that an outside observer notices in the West today. . . .
>
> Must one point out that from ancient times a decline in courage has been considered the first symptom of the end? . . .
>
> If the world has not approached its end, it has reached a major watershed in history, equal in importance to the turn from the Middle Ages to the Renaissance. It will demand from us a spiritual effort; we shall have to rise to a new height of vision.[1]

If we are ever to rise above mediocrity, we must have the vision to see beyond what the majority sees. Yet vision takes courage—courage to leave the majority behind at the foothills and scale the peaks of faith.

Living by Faith

Faith: the evidence of things not seen (see Heb. 11:1). Paul reminds us in 2 Corinthians 5:7 that, as Christians, "we walk by faith, not by sight." Since the kingdom of God is unseen, faith must be our eyes if we are ever to see beyond the material kingdom of this world.

Anxiety about our material circumstances emotionally ties us to this world—and sometimes ties us in such knots that we are bound to a life of mediocrity. In the Sermon on the Mount, Jesus cuts these bonds loose so we can soar above the majority, above mediocrity.

1. Aleksandr I. Solzhenitsyn, *East and West* (New York, N.Y.: Harper and Row, 1980), pp. 44–45, 71.

> "Do not be anxious then, saying, 'What shall we eat?' or 'What shall we drink?' or 'With what shall we clothe ourselves?' For all these things the Gentiles eagerly seek; for your heavenly Father knows that you need all these things. But seek first His kingdom and His righteousness; and all these things shall be added to you. Therefore do not be anxious for tomorrow; for tomorrow will care for itself. Each day has enough trouble of its own." (Matt. 6:31–34; see also vv. 19–21, 24)

Living by Courage

Courage: that muscle of character which flexes to give individuals, families, and nations their strength. To live above the level of mediocrity, we must live courageously. And none have lived more courageously than two men who stood up against the majority of the nation of Israel. Two men who lived by faith rather than by sight. Men of vision. Their names: Joshua and Caleb.

The Historical Context of Numbers 13–14

Set free from their bondage to Pharaoh, the Israelites gathered all their belongings and departed in a mass exodus from Egypt. Under Moses' leadership, they arrived at the edge of Canaan and, according to the last verse of Numbers 12, "camped in the wilderness of Paran"—right on the border of the Promised Land. In the Exodus, God bared His arm of salvation in a visual display of strength that should have convinced even the most spiritually nearsighted of His power: the plagues in Egypt . . . the emancipation by Pharaoh . . . the parting of the Red Sea . . . the destruction of the Egyptian army.

The Spy Mission

Now, on the border of Canaan, the Israelites could actually see the land God had promised them. Their faith was literally materializing before their very eyes. How their hearts must have raced and their spirits soared as they awaited Moses' orders! Then God instructed Moses:

> "Send out for yourself men so that they may spy out the land of Canaan, which I am going to give to the sons of Israel; you shall send a man from each of

their fathers' tribes, every one a leader among them." So Moses sent them from the wilderness of Paran at the command of the Lord, all of them men who were heads of the sons of Israel. . . .

When Moses sent them to spy out the land of Canaan, he said to them, "Go up there into the Negev; then go up into the hill country. And see what the land is like, and whether the people who live in it are strong or weak, whether they are few or many. And how is the land in which they live, is it good or bad? And how are the cities in which they live, are they like open camps or with fortifications? And how is the land, is it fat or lean? Are there trees in it or not? Make an effort then to get some of the fruit of the land." Now the time was the time of the first ripe grapes. (13:2–3, 17–20)

The Majority Report

The spies were on a reconnaissance mission. And when they returned, they had all the statistics they needed.

They brought back word to . . . all the congregation and showed them the fruit of the land. Thus they told him, and said, "We went in to the land where you sent us; and it certainly does flow with milk and honey, and this is its fruit." (vv. 26b–27)

But as sure as milk is smooth and honey is sweet, you can bet there's a bull behind the barn and bees within the hive.

"Nevertheless, the people who live in the land are strong, and the cities are fortified and very large; and moreover, we saw the descendants of Anak there. Amalek is living in the land of the Negev and the Hittites and the Jebusites and the Amorites are living in the hill country, and the Canaanites are living by the sea and by the side of the Jordan." (vv. 28–29)

In the face of these frightening facts, one man of faith had the courage to speak out against the majority.

Then Caleb quieted the people before Moses, and said, "We should by all means go up and take

> possession of it, for we shall surely overcome it." (v. 30)

But the majority—who lived by sight—pulled out their measuring sticks, which fated them to mediocrity.

> But the men who had gone up with him said, "We are not able to go up against the people, for they are too strong for us." So they gave out to the sons of Israel a bad report of the land which they had spied out, saying, "The land through which we have gone, in spying it out, is a land that devours its inhabitants; and all the people whom we saw in it are men of great size. There also we saw the Nephilim (the sons of Anak are part of the Nephilim); and we became like grasshoppers in our own sight, and so we were in their sight." (vv. 31–33)

The Reaction to the Majority Report

The Grasshoppers versus the Giants. Who do you think will win? Prediction: the Grasshoppers are gonna get squished—and get squished good! If we make our choice by sizing up the competition, shoe sizes will always win out. Likewise, the people's reaction to the report was predictably bleak.

> Then all the congregation lifted up their voices and cried, and the people wept that night. And all the sons of Israel grumbled against Moses and Aaron; and the whole congregation said to them, "Would that we had died in the land of Egypt! Or would that we had died in this wilderness! And why is the Lord bringing us into this land, to fall by the sword? Our wives and our little ones will become plunder; would it not be better for us to return to Egypt?" So they said to one another, "Let us appoint a leader and return to Egypt." (14:1–4)

Majority rules, right? After all, that's very democratic, very "of the people, by the people, for the people." But history has proven that the majority is seldom right.

The Minority Report

The majority raised a white flag. Their proposal: "When things look bleak, retreat." But a minority of two raised a different flag—

a battle flag. Their proposal: "When things look bleak, stop looking at things and start looking at God!" They had courageous vision.

> And Joshua the son of Nun and Caleb the son of Jephunneh, of those who had spied out the land, tore their clothes; and they spoke to all the congregation of the sons of Israel, saying, "The land which we passed through to spy out is an exceedingly good land. If the Lord is pleased with us, then He will bring us into this land, and give it to us—a land which flows with milk and honey. Only do not rebel against the Lord; and do not fear the people of the land, for they shall be our prey. Their protection has been removed from them, and the Lord is with us; do not fear them." (vv. 6–9)

Living by Vision

Vision: the ability to see God's presence, power, and plan in spite of the obstacles. The alphabet of vision consists of attitude, belief, capacity, determination, and enthusiasm.

- *Attitude.* When you have vision, your attitude is positive rather than negative, optimistic rather than pessimistic.
- *Belief.* "Faith is the assurance of things hoped for, the conviction of things not seen" (Heb. 11:1). When you have vision, you have assurance and confidence—not only in God, but in others and in yourself.
- *Capacity.* When you have vision, you demonstrate a willing capacity to be stretched, to do greater things than you ever dreamed you were capable of, to be a bigger person than you ever thought you could be (see Ps. 18:35–36; 119:32; Eph. 3:20).
- *Determination.* When you have vision, you develop the determination to stay at it and hold a constant focus on God, who is watching you and smiling with love at your efforts.
- *Enthusiasm.* When you have vision, you have the enthusiastic perspective that God is in your corner—fighting for you, not against you.

There's a story, perhaps familiar to you, that illustrates succinctly what vision looks like.

An American, visiting in France came upon a scene where a large church was being erected. He approached three stone masons, one after the other. Of each he asked this question: "What are you doing?" The first replied: "I'm cutting stone." The second said: "I'm cutting stone for seven francs a day." The third responded: "I'm helping to build a great cathedral."[2]

Can you see cathedrals in the challenges God has set before you—or just a lot of rough stones? Faith sees the cathedrals; sight sees only the stones.

Living Insights STUDY ONE

Knowing the outcome of a story can sometimes make us a little smug when we look at the people who had to fumble through an experience one blind step at a time. For example, how easy it is to lean back and criticize the Israelites who were afraid to enter Canaan, "Those dummies! They had walked through the Red Sea, had God with them in a pillar of cloud by day and of fire at night, ate manna every day—how could they doubt now!"

But wait a minute. What if we got more personal? What if we looked at *our* fumblings in *our* story? You know, the stretching situations and the anxiety-producing predicaments of our lives today—the ones we don't yet know the outcome of. Sort of makes any smugness fade, doesn't it?

Are you facing a Canaan now? What is your challenge? Which giants make you feel like a grasshopper?

How are you responding? With the visionary faith of Joshua

2. Jacob M. Braude, *Speaker's Encyclopedia of Stories, Quotations, and Anecdotes* (Englewood Cliffs, N.J.: Prentice-Hall, 1955), p. 400.

and Caleb or the nearsightedness of the majority of Israelites?

When we live by statistics—by comparing the odds, by numbering and measuring and weighing—the results are predictable: we become intimidated, crushed like grasshoppers by the giant heels of the challenges God has set before us.

We need to remember, though, that God gives us challenges, not to crush us, but to make us courageous.

How do you think you can transform your Canaan from a spirit-crusher to a courage-builder? Through a change in perspective, perhaps, or wanting to grow more than wanting things the way they were? Write down your ideas and insights.

As a final encouragement, take these words of one battle-tried man of God with you:

> The Lord is my light and my salvation;
> Whom shall I fear?
> The Lord is the defense of my life;
> Whom shall I dread? (Ps. 27:1)

Living Insights STUDY TWO

One of the keys to living above mediocrity is gaining spiritual vision. We spelled out the ABCs of it at the end of our chapter; now let's bring it home. In your quest for excellence, how are you doing in each of these areas? On a scale of one to five, one being a retreating Israelite and five being a courageous Caleb, rate how you think you're doing and briefly explain why. Then jot down some ideas for strengthening that aspect of your faith.

Attitude	1	2	3	4	5

____

____

____

____

Belief	1	2	3	4	5

____

____

____

____

Capacity	1	2	3	4	5

____

____

____

____

Determination	1	2	3	4	5

____

____

____

____

Enthusiasm	1	2	3	4	5

____

____

____

____

Chapter 8

DETERMINATION: DECIDING TO HANG TOUGH

Numbers 14:9–34; Joshua 14:6–13; 23:4–7; 24:14–15

Potential. We all have it in some measure. Pools of it bubble beneath the surface of our lives, like untapped reservoirs of oil. But to tap into that potential and bring it to the surface, we need to have the determination to drill. That takes not only faith enough to launch a risky venture but also persistence enough to keep drilling away, day after day, night after night—sometimes on a desolate rig.

Living above the level of mediocrity takes the determination to hang tough—whether your drilling rig is on Alaska's North Slope, on the frontier of your children's adolescent years, or in the blinding sandstorms of a marital Sahara. Excellence in life comes not so much from the gift of potential but from the guts of persistence. As President Calvin Coolidge once said,

> Press on: nothing in the world can take the place of persistence. Talent will not; nothing is more common than unsuccessful men with talent. Genius will not; unrewarded genius is almost a proverb. Education will not; the world is full of educated derelicts. Persistence and determination alone are overwhelmingly powerful.[1]

Definitions of Key Terms

Before we can drill any deeper into our topic, it is necessary to define some of the pivotal terms our study revolves around.

Vision

Vision is the ability to see beyond the majority. It is perception—finding the presence and power of God within our own circumstances. When we view life with vision, we perceive events

1. Calvin Coolidge, as quoted by Ted W. Engstrom in *Motivation to Last a Lifetime* (Grand Rapids, Mich.: Zondervan Publishing House, 1984), p. 76.

and circumstances from God's perspective. The prophet Isaiah speaks of this divine perspective in Isaiah 55, verses 8–9:

> "For My thoughts are not your thoughts,
> Neither are your ways My ways," declares the Lord.
> "For as the heavens are higher than the earth,
> So are My ways higher than your ways,
> And My thoughts than your thoughts."

When we peer through heavenly lenses, the things God views as important come into sharp relief. For example, take a look at a story in 1 Samuel 16.

King Saul had failed as a leader, so God sent Samuel to find a new king. Coming to the home of Jesse, Samuel first examined Eliab, the oldest son, for the position. Eliab's physical features were so impressive that Samuel felt sure he had found the Lord's anointed. But God corrected Samuel's blurred vision.

> "Do not look at his appearance or at the height of his stature, because I have rejected him; for God sees not as man sees, for man looks at the outward appearance, but the Lord looks at the heart." (v. 7)

Human vision focuses on externals and is easily impressed by appearances. Divine vision, on the other hand, looks beyond appearances into the hidden recesses of the heart.

Determination

Determination is faith for the long haul, disciplining ourselves to remain consistent regardless of the obstacles. A textbook example of determination can be found in the life of Daniel. Uprooted from his native land, Daniel was transplanted to the foreign soil of Babylon, where he served in King Nebuchadnezzar's court. Daniel, however, had an iron-will determination to keep himself unsullied from the pagan influences there:

> Daniel *made up his mind* that he would not defile himself. (Dan. 1:8a, emphasis added)

Dream

A dream, as we intend it, is a God-given idea, plan, agenda, or goal that leads to God-honoring results. Dreams are specific and personal, not generally applied to the public. They are the hallmark of innovative leadership.

Most of us, though, don't dream enough. We just don't take the time. What if someone were to ask you, "What are your dreams for this year? What are your hopes . . . your agenda items? What are you trusting God for?" Could you give a specific answer?

Before responding, remember to look beyond your personal goals and objectives and think about your God-given dreams. For inspiration, consider the stories of two men who dreamed great things with God's blessing.

Illustrations of Two Who Dreamed

As you may recall from our last study, we saw two men who had vision, determination, and dreams—and ten who didn't. Ten men saw the problem; two saw the solution. Ten were impressed with the size of the enemy; two were impressed with the size of their God. Ten believed victory couldn't be achieved; two believed victory would come through the promise and power of God.

Their Vision before the Fact

Joshua and Caleb's speech to the congregation concludes with vision, with their dream for the future.

> "Only do not rebel against the Lord; and do not fear the people of the land, for they shall be our prey. Their protection has been removed from them, and the Lord is with us; do not fear them." (Num. 14:9)

But so sharp is the division between the ten and the two that the majority seeks to forever silence the minority report: "All the congregation said to stone them with stones" (v. 10a). The Lord, however, intervenes in judgment against the majority.

> Then the glory of the Lord appeared in the tent of meeting to all the sons of Israel.
>
> And the Lord said to Moses, "How long will this people spurn Me? And how long will they not believe in Me, despite all the signs which I have performed in their midst? I will smite them with pestilence and dispossess them, and I will make you into a nation greater and mightier than they." (vv. 10b–12)

Moses, rather than seeking glory for himself, intercedes on behalf of the people in order to save the Lord's shining reputation from any possible tarnish before the eyes of the world.

> But Moses said to the Lord, "Then the Egyptians will hear of it, for by Thy strength Thou didst bring up this people from their midst, and they will tell it to the inhabitants of this land. They have heard that Thou, O Lord, art in the midst of this people, for Thou, O Lord, art seen eye to eye, while Thy cloud stands over them; and Thou dost go before them in a pillar of cloud by day and in a pillar of fire by night. Now if Thou dost slay this people as one man, then the nations who have heard of Thy fame will say, 'Because the Lord could not bring this people into the land which He promised them by oath, therefore He slaughtered them in the wilderness.' But now, I pray, let the power of the Lord be great, just as Thou hast declared, 'The Lord is slow to anger and abundant in lovingkindness, forgiving iniquity and transgression; but He will by no means clear the guilty, visiting the iniquity of the fathers on the children to the third and the fourth generations.' Pardon, I pray, the iniquity of this people according to the greatness of Thy lovingkindness, just as Thou also hast forgiven this people, from Egypt even until now." (vv. 13–19)

Moses' pure appeal sheathed the sharp sword of God's impending judgment (vv. 20–24). Yet, although God delayed immediate judgment, He caused the Israelites to wander in the wilderness for forty more years before entering the Promised Land—with the ultimate result that everyone who sided with the majority report died during that time (vv. 27–30a).

Ironically, the two who were to be stoned by the majority were the only men saved by God. Of the original adult population, only Joshua and Caleb were allowed to enter the Promised Land (vv. 30b–38).

Their Determination during the Fight

Now let's turn the pages of Israel's history forward to the book of Joshua. Here we'll see how Caleb and Joshua fared during the fight with the Canaanites. As we cross the threshold of this book, we leave the old, rebellious generation behind, buried in the wilderness. The new generation has invaded the land and fought their way to victory. And, just as He promised, God has given it to them.

As we come to chapter 14, the land is about to be doled out among the twelve tribes. When it is Caleb's turn to choose his parcel, he stands tall and delivers one of the most determined, visionary speeches in all of Scripture.

> "I was forty years old when Moses the servant of the Lord sent me from Kadesh-barnea to spy out the land, and I brought word back to him as it was in my heart. Nevertheless my brethren who went up with me made the heart of the people melt with fear; but I followed the Lord my God fully. So Moses swore on that day, saying, 'Surely the land on which your foot has trodden shall be an inheritance to you and to your children forever, because you have followed the Lord my God fully.' And now behold, the Lord has let me live, just as He spoke, these forty-five years, from the time that the Lord spoke this word to Moses, when Israel walked in the wilderness; and now behold, I am eighty-five years old today. I am still as strong today as I was in the day Moses sent me; as my strength was then, so my strength is now, for war and for going out and coming in. Now then, give me this hill country about which the Lord spoke on that day, for you heard on that day that Anakim were there, with great fortified cities; perhaps the Lord will be with me, and I shall drive them out as the Lord has spoken." (vv. 7–12)

When most men his age would be looking to check into a sedate retirement village, Caleb was looking for new mountains—not only to climb, but to conquer!

Do you let your age deter your dreams? Do you think such ageless visionary courage is only for those faraway Bible characters? Think again. At seventy-one, Golda Meir became prime minister of Israel. At eighty-one, Benjamin Franklin helped frame the United States Constitution. At eighty-five, Caleb rolled up his sleeves to take on the giants.

Age has nothing to do with vision, determination, or dreams.

It's *what* you do, not *when* you do it. Remember that the next time you're tempted to use your age as an excuse.

So much for Caleb. What about Joshua, the other half of this determined duo? Page forward to chapter 23, and we'll find Joshua's determination also intact as he charges God's people to stay faithful to Him.

> "Be very firm, then, to keep and do all that is written in the book of the law of Moses, so that you may not turn aside from it to the right hand or to the left, in order that you may not associate with these nations, these which remain among you, or mention the name of their gods, or make anyone swear by them, or serve them, or bow down to them." (vv. 6–7)

Unimpeded vision. Undaunted dreams. Joshua stands in his senior years as an inspiring example.

> "Now, therefore, fear the Lord and serve Him in sincerity and truth; and put away the gods which your fathers served beyond the River and in Egypt, and serve the Lord. And if it is disagreeable in your sight to serve the Lord, choose for yourselves today whom you will serve: whether the gods which your fathers served which were beyond the River, or the gods of the Amorites in whose land you are living; but as for me and my house, we will serve the Lord." (24:14–15)

Observations worth Remembering . . . Applications worth Duplicating

Several important observations and applications stand out as we come to the end of this study.

First, *age has little to do with achievement and nothing to do with commitment, so never use age as an excuse.* Both Joshua and Caleb were young men when they stood alone before their peers. Yet when they grew older, they were still standing strong, persistent in their convictions. The ranks of humanity are full of those who start well. With determination and persistence, you can also end well.

Second, *a godly walk is basic to a positive life, so never take your cues from the crowd.* Joshua and Caleb kept reiterating their full, firm commitment to the Lord. This commitment gave them both a positive outlook in the face of incredible challenges. Without divine perspective, it's easy for negativism and cynicism to creep in. Do you want to maintain a positive outlook throughout your life? Then keep the Lord, rather than the majority, as the nucleus of your motivation.

And third, *convictions are a matter of choice, not coercion, so never think your choices obligate anyone else*. In their younger years, Joshua and Caleb stood alone against a nation; in their latter years, they maintained their convictions. They stood alone and led the people, not by coercion, but by choice. When people disagreed with them, they gave them room yet still held fast to their own beliefs. May Joshua and Caleb's example encourage you to let others be responsible for their own choices, while you never quit because they disagree with you.

Living Insights — STUDY ONE

An entire generation passes, and only two men from it are still standing—men who took to heart what they had seen of God's work and therefore believed God for things He promised, which were as yet unseen.

One generation's worst expectations came true; they preferred their fears, so God gave them what they feared. Two individuals' best expectations came abundantly true; they gave their hearts fully to the Lord, so God gave them what they trusted Him for.

How can our hearts not identify with this struggle between unbelief and determined belief? Every day, it seems, we are faced with the choice, however subtle, to trust God or trust our own ideas of what's best. This choice, as we have seen, carries with it somber, inescapable consequences.

Rather than answer two or three questions and go on to the next study, stop here and meditate on their examples—both Caleb's and Joshua's as well as the perishing Israelites'. Read again their words and God's from Numbers 14 and Joshua 14, 23, and 24, perhaps from a different translation—one that's unfamiliar to your ear and therefore fresh in its impact and meaning. Write down the phrases that pierce through your heart and mind, that teach you with life-changing truth.

Then pray about the faith choices you make each day; pray to your Father who is "slow to anger and abundant in lovingkindness, forgiving iniquity and transgression; but [who] will by no means clear the guilty" (Num. 14:18). If your heart struggles with unbelief, ask Him to help you determine to transform it into a believing heart, a seeing heart, a trusting heart (see Mark 9:24). The outcome is of the greatest importance.

Living Insights STUDY TWO

How do the three concluding observations from our study apply to you? Do you agree with them? Do any of them confront self-imposed barriers to following God in your life? Which strikes closest to home with you? Why? Take time to interact with each of these statements more deeply.

- Age has little to do with achievement and nothing to do with commitment.

- A godly life is basic to a positive outlook.

- Convictions are a matter of choice, not coercion.

Based on your responses, what does your determination to hold on to your faith in God look like?

Chapter 9

PRIORITIES: DETERMINING WHAT COMES FIRST

Matthew 6:33; Colossians 1:13–18; Luke 14:15–33

Robert Frost's poem "The Road Not Taken" describes two roads discovered during a walk in the woods. Frost knows he can only explore one, and he tells himself that someday he will travel the other. But, realistically, he knows he will never return. And by the time we reach the end of the poem, we realize the poet is talking about something infinitely more important than a simple choice of paths.

> I shall be telling this with a sigh
> Somewhere ages and ages hence:
> Two roads diverged in a wood, and I—
> I took the one less traveled by,
> And that has made all the difference.[1]

No, Frost is not talking about the choice of paths in a wood, but the choice of paths in a person's life. Choosing a road symbolizes any choice we must make between alternatives that appear equally attractive but lead to entirely different destinations.

Whether you arrive at excellence or mediocrity depends upon the choices you make at the crossroads. And your priorities will function as signposts to help you determine which road you will travel.

A Reminder of Unseen Values

Priorities not only point the way, they also reveal the values that often hide beneath the surface of our lives. As the Israelites hesitated at a confusing crossroads, Joshua challenged them to make a choice. Then, charting the straight-and-narrow path to God, Joshua revealed his priorities and values:

1. Robert Frost, "The Road Not Taken," from *Complete Poems of Robert Frost*, copyright 1930, 1947, 1949 by Holt, Rinehart and Winston; copyright 1936, 1942 by Robert Frost. Reprinted by permission in *The Pocket Book of Modern Verse*, 3d ed., rev. (New York, N.Y.: Pocket Books, 1972), p. 180.

> "And if it is disagreeable in your sight to serve the Lord, choose for yourselves today whom you will serve: whether the gods which your fathers served which were beyond the River, or the gods of the Amorites in whose land you are living; but as for me and my house, we will serve the Lord." (Josh. 24:15)

Joshua knew that service could not be rendered to two masters, because divided loyalties cannot maintain their balance for long. A shift in the center of gravity will always take place—our loyalties will always lean toward one side or the other. This is precisely what Jesus tells us in the Sermon on the Mount.

> "No one can serve two masters; for either he will hate the one and love the other, or he will hold to one and despise the other. You cannot serve God and mammon." (Matt. 6:24)

Because our master is God, Jesus exhorts us to let any concern for our provision fall on His shoulders rather than let it take over the top spot on our list of priorities.

> "For this reason I say to you, do not be anxious for your life, as to what you shall eat, or what you shall drink; nor for your body, as to what you shall put on. Is not life more than food, and the body than clothing?" (v. 25)

He concludes by showing us our Master's benevolence and how that should affect the way we order our priorities.

> "For all these things the Gentiles eagerly seek;[2] for your heavenly Father knows that you need all these things. But seek first His kingdom and His righteousness; and all these things shall be added to you." (vv. 32–33)

A Revelation of Absolute Authority

Logically, God *should* have first place in our lives, because He created us and is our absolute authority.

2. The Greek word is *epizēteō* and means "to search, to strive for, to desire strongly." The verb's action is continuous and implies "to keep on striving for, keep on searching after, keep on desiring."

> For He delivered us from the domain of darkness, and transferred us to the kingdom of His beloved Son, in whom we have redemption, the forgiveness of sins. And He is the image of the invisible God, the first-born of all creation. For by Him all things were created, both in the heavens and on earth, visible and invisible, whether thrones or dominions or rulers or authorities—all things have been created by Him and for Him. And He is before all things, and in Him all things hold together. He is also head of the body, the church; and He is the beginning, the first-born from the dead; so that He Himself might come to have first place in everything. (Col. 1:13–18)

First place in everything. Everything? Everything! That's His proper place. That's what it means to have Jesus as Lord of your life. Does He have first place in everything in your life?

If you're dating someone, does Jesus have first place in that relationship? Or is that relationship competing for your loyalty to the Savior and causing you to make moral compromises? If you're involved in a business, is Jesus chairman of the board? Or do economic considerations veto His principles? If you're a homemaker, is Jesus the person around whom you're making your home? Or is He low on your list of priorities, somewhere after grocery shopping and cleaning the kitchen?

A Response of Incredible Relevance

At a dinner party recorded in Luke 14:15–24, Jesus tells a parable about priorities.

> "A certain man was giving a big dinner, and he invited many; and at the dinner hour he sent his slave to say to those who had been invited, 'Come; for everything is ready now.'" (vv. 16–17)

If the host in this parable had been important enough to those invited, they would have made his dinner a top priority. But because he was not first in their lives, other interests wrested their attention.

> "But they all alike began to make excuses. The first one said to him, 'I have bought a piece of land and

> I need to go out and look at it; please consider me excused.' And another one said, 'I have bought five yoke of oxen, and I am going to try them out; please consider me excused.' And another one said, 'I have married a wife, and for that reason I cannot come.'" (vv. 18–20)

Property . . . possessions . . . passion. These priorities came first with the invited guests. Inherently, these things are not wrong. But they are designed to serve us, not rule us. When they are subservient to our love for the Lord, they're good. But as masters, they dominate our lesser priorities with an iron hand.

As a result of the feeble RSVP attempts by his intended guests, the host sent out another invitation—this time to people who were willing to rearrange their priorities.

> "And the slave came back and reported this to his master. Then the head of the household became angry and said to his slave, 'Go out at once into the streets and lanes of the city and bring in here the poor and crippled and blind and lame.' And the slave said, 'Master, what you commanded has been done, and still there is room.' And the master said to the slave, 'Go out into the highways and along the hedges, and compel them to come in, that my house may be filled. For I tell you, none of those men who were invited shall taste of my dinner.'" (vv. 21–24)

Contextually and historically, the parable refers to the gospel invitation that was refused by the Jews and was extended instead to the Gentiles. As such, it illustrates in story form the truth of John 1:11–12.

> He came to His own, and those who were His own did not receive Him. But as many as received Him, to them He gave the right to become children of God, even to those who believe in His name.

But the parable of the slighted host applies to us today as well. If we're too preoccupied with other priorities, then we can hardly expect to enjoy the feast of fellowship He has offered to those who put Him first.

A Review of Personal Priorities

Immediately following the parable, in Luke 14:25–35, Jesus thins the multitudes with a short course on personal priorities. Placing Him first in their lives would preclude competition from any other loyalty. No relationship—however intimate—can compete with Christ for first place in our hearts.

> "If anyone comes to Me, and does not hate his own father and mother and wife and children and brothers and sisters, yes, and even his own life, he cannot be My disciple." (v. 26)

And no possession—however prized—can come between you and the Lord.

> "So therefore, no one of you can be My disciple who does not give up all his own possessions." (v. 33)

Following Christ means taking the road "less traveled"—and that road leads to Calvary.

> "Whoever does not carry his own cross and come after Me cannot be My disciple." (v. 27)

In the final analysis, at every decision, two roads stretch before us—roads that intersect but lead to totally different destinations. The popular one is the way of self . . . leading to the dense, entangling overgrowth of ego. The other is the way of the cross . . . the less-traveled path that leads to the green pastures of intimate fellowship with Christ. I hope our study has encouraged you to make Jesus the number one priority of your life. And I hope you will be able to say with a satisfied sigh somewhere ages and ages hence:

> Two roads diverged in a wood, and I—
> I took the one less traveled by,
> And that has made all the difference.

Living Insights STUDY ONE

"We're number one!" is the competitive chant of every athletic team, every corporation, every nation. Even churches get into the cheerleading act when they tout Sunday school attendance, conversions, or a multiplicity of projects and programs.

Egoism is really at the root of our priorities, isn't it? It's difficult to put anything in front of *our* careers, *our* goals, *our* desires. It's difficult because, in reality, *we* are number one.

Now, that may be a hard pill to swallow, but if the diagnosis is correct, then for our own sakes we'd better just get a tall glass of water and gulp it down.

Who or what is number one in your life? Before you rattle off a pious list of priorities, be honest with yourself about what dominates your thoughts, your dreams, your ambitions, your finances, your time.

Are your priorities in the right order?

If not, what do you need to do to rearrange them to "seek first His kingdom"?

Living Insights STUDY TWO

Our priorities reveal what's important to us. Whatever or whoever is in first place—if it isn't Christ and His kingdom, it is in the wrong place. This study included one of the most important passages in the Bible—Matthew 6:33. If you've never done so, memorize this verse today. If you already have, choose another from our study that speaks of putting Christ first. The key to memory work is repetition. Read the verse aloud, and write it out several times. You'll soon discover that the verse has become yours.

Chapter 10

ACCOUNTABILITY: ANSWERING THE HARD QUESTIONS

Selected Scriptures

Plato said in his work *Apology*: "The life which is unexamined is not worth living."[1] Self-examination is painful enough, let alone scrutiny by others. The reason is uncovered by the noted writer Samuel Coleridge.

> The most frequent impediment to men's turning the mind inward upon themselves is that they are afraid of what they shall find there. There is an aching hollowness in the bosom, a dark cold speck at the heart, an obscure and boding sense of something that must be kept *out of sight* of the conscience; some secret lodger, whom they can neither resolve to reject nor retain.[2]

However piercing, inspection by self, others, and God is the refining process through which our hearts are kept pure. David was known as a man after God's heart (Acts 13:22), not because he was perfect, but because he acknowledged God's diagnostic scrutiny—he was always willing to crawl onto the operating table for God's exploratory surgery. This was the redeeming characteristic of his life. Notice, for example, how he begins and ends this psalm:

> O Lord, Thou hast searched me and known me.
> Thou dost know when I sit down and when
> I rise up;
> Thou dost understand my thought from afar.
> Thou dost scrutinize my path and my lying down,
> And art intimately acquainted with all my ways.
> Even before there is a word on my tongue,

1. Plato, as quoted in *Bartlett's Familiar Quotations*, 15th ed., rev. and enl., ed. Emily Morison Beck (Boston, Mass.: Little, Brown and Co., 1980), p. 83.

2. Samuel Coleridge, *Aids to Reflection*, as quoted in *Handbook of Preaching Resources from Literature*, ed. James D. Robertson (Grand Rapids, Mich.: Baker Book House, 1962), p. 189.

Behold, O Lord, Thou dost know it all. . . .
Search me, O God, and know my heart;
Try me and know my anxious thoughts;
And see if there be any hurtful way in me,
And lead me in the everlasting way.
(Ps. 139:1–4, 23–24)

That's fiber-optic scrutiny. That's a man whose heart is laid bare before the master surgeon's knife. That, in a word, is accountability.

The Essence of Excellence

We, too, can model David's excellence before the Lord if we will cultivate four key qualities.

A Review of Three Essentials

First, people who live above the level of mediocrity and impact others are people of *vision*. Vision is the ability to see above and beyond the majority—to be unimpressed by the statistics, unintimidated by the odds, and unhindered by the obstacles.

Second, people who impact others model *determination*. Determination is nothing more than the bulldog tenacity to tough it out through thick or thin. It trudges onward, no matter how rigorous the road, how rough the rocks, how steep the slope, or how dangerous the drop-off.

Third, those who bypass the highway of mediocrity for the less-traveled road to excellence are people with their *priorities* in proper perspective—people who place eternal price tags on all their relationships, work, and possessions.

A Fourth Essential

People who breathe the rare mountain air of excellence are those who have learned the wisdom of *accountability*. Accountability is trusting your life to a few carefully selected, loyal confidants who love you—confidants who have the right to examine, question, appraise, and give counsel. Like ropes for a mountain climber, these people hold your life in check and keep you from slipping precipitously to destruction.

Accountability has four sister qualities:

1. *Vulnerability*—lowering your defensive walls, even if it means exposure to possible pain.

2. *Teachability*—being willing to learn no matter how difficult the assignment.
3. *Availability*—being on call night or day for God's purposes.
4. *Honesty*—being open to the truth no matter how revealing.

A Scriptural Analysis of Accountability

In our society, privacy is a perk that goes along with promotion. Lack of accountability is considered the height of success—it is achievement's carte blanche. Yet unaccountability, whether it's in the Oval Office or in a country store, is unwise. And not only unwise but unbiblical.

Biblical Principles

There are three major principles in support of accountability. First: *Accountability to God is inevitable and inescapable.*

> But you, why do you judge your brother? Or you again, why do you regard your brother with contempt? For *we shall all stand before the judgment seat of God.* For it is written,
> "As I live, says the Lord, every knee shall bow to Me,
> And every tongue shall give praise to God."
> So then *each one of us shall give account of himself to God.* (Rom. 14:10–12, emphasis added)

Each of us will be held accountable to God not only for our actions but for every word as well.

> "The good man out of his good treasure brings forth what is good; and the evil man out of his evil treasure brings forth what is evil. And I say to you, that every careless word that men shall speak, they shall render account for it in the day of judgment." (Matt. 12:35–36)

Second: *Accountability to spiritual leaders is commanded by God and profitable to us.* Most of us have no argument with being accountable to God—the all-knowing, all-wise, all-powerful. The rub occurs when the awesome task of keeping us in line is handed over to ordinary human beings. But, as in Paul's conclusion to 1 Corinthians, the believers are exhorted to be responsible to the church's leaders.

> Now I urge you, brethren (you know the household of Stephanas, that they were the first fruits of Achaia, and that they have devoted themselves for ministry to the saints), that you also be in subjection to such men and to everyone who helps in the work and labors. (16:15–16)

The rationale for such measures of accountability is found in Hebrews 13:17:

> Obey your leaders, and submit to them; for they keep watch over your souls, as those who will give an account. Let them do this with joy and not with grief, for this would be unprofitable for you.

As believers, we are not islands, not dots of humanity in some unconnected archipelago. We are part of a vast continent known as the church. We need each other, decidedly—and sometimes desperately.

Third: *Accountability to one another is helpful and healthy.* When one member of the body of Christ is weak, the stronger members should be there to help build that person up.

> Now we who are strong ought to bear the weaknesses of those without strength and not just please ourselves. Let each of us please his neighbor for his good, to his edification. (Rom. 15:1–2)

When sin disjoints a member of the body, those who are healthy are responsible to set the broken bone with a physician's firm but gentle touch.

> Brethren, even if a man is caught in any trespass, you who are spiritual, restore such a one in a spirit of gentleness; each one looking to yourself, lest you too be tempted. Bear one another's burdens, and thus fulfill the law of Christ. (Gal. 6:1–2)

Historical Examples

Let's take a quick safari through the Scriptures in order to find a few trophies of accountability to hang on our mental walls. Blazing Old Testament trails, we find Joseph accountable to Potiphar

(Gen. 39); Saul to Samuel (1 Sam. 13); King David to the prophet Nathan (2 Sam. 12); Nehemiah, as cupbearer, to the king (Neh. 1–2); and Daniel to his peers and several kings (Dan. 1; 5; 6).

Crossing the New Testament boundary, we find Jesus as the epitome of accountability (see John 16:28; 17:4; Heb. 5:8). Following His example, the disciples were accountable to Jesus and later to one another; John Mark was accountable to Paul and later to Barnabas; Paul and Barnabas, in turn, were accountable to the church at Antioch; and Timothy was accountable to Paul, his father in the faith. Of course, like a flat rock skipping across the water, we've barely touched the surface of scriptural examples.

Practical Advantages

From the encouragement of biblical models let's now turn to the instruction of scriptural principles. Proverbs itemizes for us the practical advantages of accountability.

1. *When we are accountable, we're less likely to stumble into a trap.*

> Where there is no guidance, the people fall,
> But in abundance of counselors there is victory. (11:14)

> The teaching of the wise is a fountain of life,
> To turn aside from the snares of death. (13:14)

> Poverty and shame will come to him who neglects discipline,
> But he who regards reproof will be honored. (v. 18)

> He who walks with wise men will be wise,
> But the companion of fools will suffer harm. (v. 20)

> He whose ear listens to the life-giving reproof
> Will dwell among the wise.
> He who neglects discipline despises himself,
> But he who listens to reproof acquires understanding. (15:31–32)

2. *When we are accountable, we are more likely to see the whole picture.* Most of us go through life like a horse with blinders: we see the path directly before us, but we're oblivious to the periphery. Friends to whom we're accountable not only remove our blinders to give us a more panoramic view, they also sharpen

our vision so we can see our own blind spots.

> Iron sharpens iron,
> So one man sharpens another. . . .
> As in water face reflects face,
> So the heart of man reflects man. (27:17, 19)

3. *When we are accountable, we are not likely to get away with sinful and unwise actions.*

> Faithful are the wounds of a friend,
> But deceitful are the kisses of an enemy. (v. 6)

In a nutshell, accountability should be based on caring relationships—with friends who know us well enough to tell us the truth and love us enough to tell it with their arms around our shoulders. One poet eloquently expressed the inestimable value of such friendship.

> Oh, the comfort—the inexpressible comfort of
> feeling safe with a person,
> Having neither to weigh thoughts,
> Nor measure words—but pouring them
> All right out—just as they are—
> Chaff and grain together—
> Certain that a faithful hand will
> Take and sift them—
> Keep what is worth keeping—
> And with the breath of kindness
> Blow the rest away.[3]

A Probing Examination of Ourselves

Such a topic as accountability can't be left in the theoretical; it needs to be taken into the very personal arena of our lives. So, in the quiet privacy of your soul, ask yourself the following questions concerning accountability in your life.

- Can you name one or more people outside your family to whom you've made yourself accountable?

3. Dinah Maria Mulock Craik, as quoted in *Handbook of Preaching Resources from Literature*, p. 71. An excellent book on building this type of friendship is *The Friendship Factor*, by Alan Loy McGinnis (Minneapolis, Minn.: Augsburg Publishing House, 1979).

- Are you aware of the dangers of unaccountability particular to your life?
- When is the last time you gave an account for the private areas of your life to someone outside your family?

Remember, accountability is not a long, bony finger of accusation pointed your way; it is the arm around your shoulder of someone who cares enough about *you* to help you stay in "the everlasting way" (Ps. 139:24). Won't you open your life to this safeguard of excellence?

Living Insights STUDY ONE

Proverbs warns us that "Pride goes before destruction, And a haughty spirit before stumbling" (16:18).

Yet pride often accompanies a climb to the top. When we scale the peaks of personal, financial, or corporate success, pride stands there beside us, looking down on those we left behind—those panting at the tree line, blistered on the foothills, cowering in the valley.

When looking down on others with self-satisfied smugness, we can become careless in our footing and forget that a disastrous fall is only a step away. But if people who love us are anchoring our ascent, their ropes can keep us in check and prevent us from stumbling to destruction.

How sure are your ropes of accountability? If, upon your inspection at the conclusion of our chapter, they seemed alarmingly frayed, take this time to weave together some positive strands of action that will strengthen them.

What are the names of some people outside your family to whom you could be accountable?

What do you need to do to transform the particular dangers you face by remaining unaccountable into safe, healthy, and excellent ways of living?

How can you make accountability more of a natural, regular part of your life?

____

____

____

As you're climbing toward excellence, remember the perils at the peaks—and remember to have people above and below you holding the ropes.

Living Insights STUDY TWO

If we are going to live above the level of mediocrity, we must make sure we've firmly cemented in our minds and lives the principles we've studied. Listed below, then, are the titles of our first ten studies. In the space provided, record the most meaningful truths, insights, and applications you have discovered from each.

LIVING ABOVE THE LEVEL OF MEDIOCRITY

Confronting Mediocrity Takes Thinking Clearly

It Starts in Your Mind (Part One) ______________________

____

____

It Starts in Your Mind (Part Two) ______________________

____

____

It Involves His Kingdom (Part One) ____________________

____

____

It Involves His Kingdom (Part Two) ____________________

____

____

It Costs Your Commitment ______________________________

____

____

It Calls for Extravagant Love ______________________________

____

____

Overcoming Mediocrity Means Living Differently

Vision: Seeing beyond the Majority ______________________________

____

____

Determination: Deciding to Hang Tough ______________________________

____

____

Priorities: Determining What Comes First ______________________________

____

____

Accountability: Answering the Hard Questions ______________________________

____

____

Part Three

Combating Mediocrity Requires Fighting Fiercely

Chapter 11

WINNING THE BATTLE OVER GREED

Luke 12:13–34

In his classic work *The Decline and Fall of the Roman Empire*, Edward Gibbon noted: "Avarice is an insatiate and universal passion."[1]

His words echo the sentiments Solomon expressed in Ecclesiastes: "He who loves money will not be satisfied with money, nor he who loves abundance with its income. This too is vanity" (5:10).

The Greeks used an interesting word when referring to greed. It meant "a thirst for having more."[2] Picture a shipwrecked sailor on a life raft in the middle of an ocean. His terrible thirst impels him to drink the salt water, but it only makes him thirstier. This causes him to drink even more, which makes him thirstier still. He consumes more and more of the salty water . . . until, paradoxically, he becomes dehydrated and dies.

Greed is like that—unquenchable, insatiable. And deadly.

Several Faces of Greed

Greed—an inordinate desire for more—is an untamed beast that claws and clutches in a craving thirst to possess. The word *enough* is not in this beast's vocabulary. A glutton, forever hungry, it can only cry out: "more . . . MORE . . . MORE!" Greed's hideous face wears many masks, which only thinly disguise its ravenous nature.

First: *Greed is an excessive motivation to have more money*. Like Dickens' Ebenezer Scrooge—"a squeezing, wrenching, grasping, scraping, clutching, covetous old sinner!"[3]—greed is a hoarding desire for money. It touches the Midas in us all and gilds our souls with brittle, suffocating gold leaf.

Second: *Greed is an excessive determination to own more things*. This second mask is material possessions—an obsessive compulsion

1. Edward Gibbon, as quoted in *Great Treasury of Western Thought*, ed. Mortimer J. Adler and Charles Van Doren (New York, N.Y.: R. R. Bowker Co., 1977), p. 299.

2. From the word *pleonexia*, translated "greed" in Luke 12:15.

3. Charles Dickens, *A Christmas Carol* (New York, N.Y.: Dial Books, 1983), p. 12.

for more clothes, bigger closets; more china, bigger cabinets; more cars, bigger garages; more furniture, bigger houses.

Third: *Greed is an excessive desire to become more famous, to make a name for oneself.* This third is the mask of fame. Greed covets the lifestyles of not only the rich but the famous as well. From Narcissus in Greek mythology to Norma Desmond in the film *Sunset Boulevard*, this face is constantly surrounding itself with the mirrors and memorabilia of ego.

Fourth: *Greed is an excessive need to gain more control.* The fourth masquerade is manipulation. Always wanting to be coach instead of player . . . chairman of the board instead of stockholder . . . queen bee instead of drone. Rather than serve, greed seeks to be the one who is served, the one in control.

Greed Exposed and Denounced

Luke 12 preserves a picture of greed's second mask, framed in a parable. In it Jesus, the bottomless well of living water, gives advice on avarice that finally quenches our soul's innermost thirst.

The Dialogue

The catalyst to this parable is the urgent imperative of a greedy man.

> And someone in the crowd said to Him, "Teacher, tell my brother to divide the family inheritance with me." But He said to him, "Man, who appointed Me a judge or arbiter over you?" (vv. 13–14)

Although Jesus refuses to referee the man's family affairs, He uses the intrusive request to introduce a short sermon. In doing so, Jesus expounds a principle that sounds a warning against our enemy, greed.

A Principle

Turning from one man's problem to the broader problem of all people, Jesus shifts His attention from the greedy brother and addresses the whole crowd.

> And He said to them, "Beware, and be on your guard against every form of greed; for not even when one has an abundance does his life consist of his possessions." (v. 15)

Jesus warns the crowd not to let the masqueraded faces of greed fool them into thinking that life can be reduced to a banker's balance sheet. To illustrate this principle, He tells a parable.

The Parable

> "The land of a certain rich man was very productive. And he began reasoning to himself, saying, 'What shall I do, since I have no place to store my crops?' And he said, 'This is what I will do: I will tear down my barns and build larger ones, and there I will store all my grain and my goods. And I will say to my soul, "Soul, you have many goods laid up for many years to come; take your ease, eat, drink and be merry."' But God said to him, 'You fool! This very night your soul is required of you; and now who will own what you have prepared?' So is the man who lays up treasure for himself, and is not rich toward God." (vv. 16–21)

A bumper-crop harvest but a bankrupt heart. What went wrong? Where did this man's plow take a wrong turn?

First, *he didn't know himself*. This man put all his eggs in the basket of the here and now, only to have them broken in an up-ending brush with the hereafter. He was a man who really didn't know what satisfied his soul. He labored under the distortion that ultimate satisfaction in life is derived from the creature comforts of ease, epicurean delights, and entertainment. Yet what he didn't know was that, like the rippled image of the moon on a lake, these pleasures were only reflections of the much higher, brighter pleasure of God Himself.

It is in the light of this greater pleasure that all our lesser pleasures find their illumination, as Solomon noted:

> There is nothing better for a man than to eat and drink and tell himself that his labor is good. This also I have seen, that it is from the hand of God. For who can eat and who can have enjoyment without Him? (Eccles. 2:24–25)

Second, *he didn't care about other people*. The man's remarks are thoroughly and unashamedly full of himself. Count the *I*'s and *my*'s in the parable. A total of eleven! Sounds like the self-indulgence of Solomon in Ecclesiastes 2:1–11. Look at the parable again. Count the *they*'s, *them*'s, and *their*'s. Not one! Because this man didn't care about the *they, them,* and *their*; he cared only about the *I*, *me*, and *my*. Greed can often hide behind the first person pronoun.

Third, *he didn't make room for God.* The man worried about not having adequate storage for his crops. What he should have worried about was that he had no room in his life for God. His silos were marked "Grain Only"; he had no space for spiritual things, no place in his heart for God.

A Series of Truths

On the basis of this story, Jesus presented what appears to be something of a *Reader's Digest* condensed version of the Sermon on the Mount.

> And He said to His disciples, "For this reason I say to you, do not be anxious for your life, as to what you shall eat; nor for your body, as to what you shall put on. For life is more than food, and the body than clothing. Consider the ravens, for they neither sow nor reap; and they have no storeroom nor barn; and yet God feeds them; how much more valuable you are than the birds! And which of you by being anxious can add a single cubit to his life's span? If then you cannot do even a very little thing, why are you anxious about other matters? Consider the lilies, how they grow; they neither toil nor spin; but I tell you, even Solomon in all his glory did not clothe himself like one of these. But if God so arrays the grass in the field, which is alive today and tomorrow is thrown into the furnace, how much more will He clothe you, O men of little faith! And do not seek what you shall eat, and what you shall drink, and do not keep worrying. For all these things the nations of the world eagerly seek; but your Father knows that you need these things. But seek for His kingdom, and these things shall be added to you. Do not be afraid, little flock, for your Father has chosen gladly to give you the kingdom. Sell your possessions and give to charity; make yourselves purses which do not wear out, an unfailing treasure

> in heaven, where no thief comes near, nor moth destroys. For where your treasure is, there will your heart be also." (Luke 12:22–34)

From this homily on the heart, we can gather enough truth to fill four concluding baskets.

1. Those who lose the battle with greed are characterized by anxiety and a pursuit of the temporal (vv. 22–23).
2. Those who win the battle over greed realize their value in God's sight and simply trust Him (vv. 24–30).
3. Overcoming greed requires deliberate and assertive action (vv. 31–33).
4. Real valuables are sealed in our hearts (v. 34).

Does greed have you clutching for money . . . material possessions . . . fame . . . control? Like Jesus in Gethsemane, won't you loosen your grip on life and submit, empty-handed, to God's will? In raising your empty hands to God, you will find a fullness you never knew existed.

> One by one He took them from me,
> All the things I valued most,
> Until I was empty-handed;
> Every glittering toy was lost,
>
> And I walked earth's highway, grieving,
> In my rags and poverty.
> Till I heard His voice inviting,
> "Lift your empty hands to Me!"
>
> So I held my hands toward Heaven,
> And He filled them with a store
> Of His own transcendent riches
> Till they could contain no more.
>
> And at last I comprehended
> With my stupid mind and dull,
> That God COULD not pour His riches
> Into hands already full![4]

4. Martha Snell Nicholson, "Treasures," in *Ivory Palaces* (Wilmington, Calif.: Martha Snell Nicholson, 1946), p. 67.

Living Insights STUDY ONE

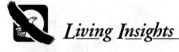

Greed has many faces—one that's driven to get more money at whatever the cost to oneself or others; another that's hungry to amass more and more possessions; one whose craving eyes shine in the spotlight of fame; and still another that endlessly schemes to gain control and wield power over other people's lives.

And sometimes, its face looks startlingly like our own.

Do you struggle with greed? Which of the four faces we peered into in this chapter most resembles yours? How have you noticed this in your life?

____

____

____

____

A face like greed's can't be fixed with a mere makeover or even drastic plastic surgery. This kind can only be changed from the inside out (see Mark 7:21–23). Fortunately, God has given us two means of doing just that: His Word and His Holy Spirit.

As you read the following Scripture passages, open yourself to the Spirit's leading. You will very likely find a truth or two that will help you make a complete about-face!

Proverbs 23:4–5 ______________________________

____

____

Matthew 6:19–34 ______________________________

____

____

Matthew 16:26 ________________________________

____

____

Philippians 4:10–13 ______________________________

____

____

Colossians 3:1–17 ______________________________

____

____

1 Timothy 6:1–19 ______________________________

____

____

Living Insights STUDY TWO

Did you realize that you could be greedy and not even know it? Many of us are blind to our own avaricious shortcomings. Here's a surefire method for detecting this weakness.

Greed can be spotted by employing a principle we learned in our last lesson—accountability. Do you have someone to whom you can be accountable? Someone who knows you well enough to say the hard things to you? If so, ask this person to tell you about any greed showing up in your life. It may be difficult, but it's essential for your spiritual growth. And it's essential in your battle against mediocrity.

Chapter 12

Slaying the Dragon of Traditionalism

Luke 5:27–39

Passivity is the surest formula for mediocrity. Sit back complacently, and the world will squeeze you into its mold faster than a waffle iron makes waffles (compare Rom. 12:2a). And as the waffle iron turns out monotonously uniform waffles, one after another, so the world mass-produces people according to the mold of mediocrity.

For the Christian, that waffle iron is traditionalism—rituals that have become rigidly set into a cast-iron matrix of rules and regulations. Traditionalism not only squeezes you into its mold, it forever leaves its imprint scorched on your life, like batter seared by the iron.

If you're ever to escape the molding influence of this world, you can't sit around in a room-temperature state of lethargy. Poet e. e. cummings expressed it well:

> To be nobody but yourself in a world which is doing its best, night and day, to make you everybody else, means to fight the hardest battle which any human being can fight; and never stop fighting.[1]

To combat mediocrity, a backbone has to emerge from the spineless batter of passivity. You have to stand up and resist. We're not talking cream puffs here. We're talking about a courageous knight who dons his armor, mounts his charger, takes up his shield, and brandishes his lance in a heroic quest to slay a dragon—the fire-breathing dragon of traditionalism.

Identifying the Dragon

Traditions, in and of themselves, are not bad. In fact, the right kind of traditions are good and healthy—traditions with a solid network of reliable truth that put us in touch with our roots. Paul exhorts us to "stand firm and hold to the traditions which you were

1. e. e. cummings, as quoted by Luci Swindoll in *You Bring the Confetti* (Waco, Tex.: Word Books, 1986), pp. 35–36.

taught" (2 Thess. 2:15). Conversely, he commands us to "keep aloof from every brother who leads an unruly life and not according to the tradition which you received from us" (3:6).

However, a great deal of difference exists between *tradition* and *traditionalism*. Jaroslav Pelikan put his finger on the distinction when he observed:

> Tradition is the living faith of the dead, traditionalism is the dead faith of the living.[2]

By *traditionalism* we mean an attitude that resists change, adaptation, or alteration. It clutches tradition so tightly that the blood supply to our spiritual brain is cut off, distorting vision and blurring the distinction between custom and commandment. Traditionalism is suspicious and censorious of the new, the innovative, the different. It substitutes a stuffy, legalistic system for the Spirit's freedom and freshness, law for liberty, rules for renovation, regulations for renewal. In Mark 7, Jesus rebukes the Pharisees for confusing human custom with divine command.

> And the Pharisees and some of the scribes gathered together around Him when they had come from Jerusalem, and had seen that some of His disciples were eating their bread with impure hands, that is, unwashed. (For the Pharisees and all the Jews do not eat unless they carefully wash their hands, thus observing the traditions of the elders; and when they come from the market place, they do not eat unless they cleanse themselves; and there are many other things which they have received in order to observe, such as the washing of cups and pitchers and copper pots.) And the Pharisees and the scribes asked Him, "Why do Your disciples not walk according to the tradition of the elders, but eat their bread with impure hands?" And He said to them, "Rightly did Isaiah prophesy of you hypocrites, as it is written,
>
> 'This people honors Me with their lips,
> But their heart is far away from Me.

2. Jaroslav Pelikan, *The Vindication of Tradition* (New Haven, Conn.: Yale University Press, 1984), p. 65.

> But in vain do they worship Me,
> Teaching as doctrines the precepts of men.'
>
> Neglecting the commandment of God, you hold to the tradition of men." (vv. 1–8)

First-Century Traditionalism

In Jesus' day the dragon of traditionalism reared its ugly head from the catacombs of Pharisaism—so much so that traditionalism and Pharisaism became virtually synonymous. In Luke 5, we see the Pharisees pressing their smug traditional noses against the dining room windows of a tax-gatherer named Levi.

The Parlor

Levi had apparently become a believer and left his lucrative job as a tax-collector to follow Christ (vv. 27–28). To introduce his friends to Jesus, Levi holds an open-house reception.

> And Levi gave a big reception for Him in his house; and there was a great crowd of tax-gatherers and other people who were reclining at the table with them. And the Pharisees and their scribes began grumbling at His disciples, saying, "Why do you eat and drink with the tax-gatherers and sinners?" And Jesus answered and said to them, "It is not those who are well who need a physician, but those who are sick. I have not come to call the righteous but sinners to repentance." (vv. 29–32)

The indignation of the scribes and Pharisees gives Jesus an innovative opportunity to instruct—directly, with a principle; and indirectly, with a parable.

The Principle

These formal stuffed shirts simply can't handle the festive freedom of Christ's disciples.

> And they said to Him, "The disciples of John often fast and offer prayers; the disciples of the Pharisees also do the same; but Yours eat and drink." (v. 33)

In responding, Jesus states an important principle: *There's a time to fast and a time to feast.*

> And Jesus said to them, "You cannot make the attendants of the bridegroom fast while the bridegroom is with them, can you? But the days will come; and when the bridegroom is taken away from them, then they will fast in those days." (vv. 34–35)

As long as the bridegroom is present, it's time for merriment, not mourning. It's a time to celebrate . . . to laugh . . . to dance . . . to sing . . . to dine. Later on, when He's gone, that's the time to fast.

The Parable

Jesus postscripts this principle with a parable—a parable that, like "Auld Lang Syne," rings out the old era and brings in the new. To do this, Jesus uses two common word pictures.

The new patch and the old garment. The first illustration is homespun.

> "No one tears a piece from a new garment and puts it on an old garment; otherwise he will both tear the new, and the piece from the new will not match the old." (v. 36)

Anyone who grew up with unshrunk denim jeans and 100 percent cotton shirts can easily decipher this parable. Patch an old, shrunken garment with a new, unwashed piece of cloth and the patch will pull away from the garment when it's washed.

Here, the old garments are the hand-me-downs of traditionalism. In an attempt to iron out the interpretation of God's Law, the Pharisees had added over six hundred new wrinkles. Like too much starch added to the wash, these rigid rules chafed the very people they sought to clothe.

The new wine and the old wineskins. Here Jesus changes to a more festive metaphor.

> "And no one puts new wine into old wineskins; otherwise the new wine will burst the skins, and it will be spilled out, and the skins will be ruined. But new wine must be put into fresh wineskins. And no one, after drinking old wine wishes for new; for he says, 'The old is good enough.'" (vv. 37–39)

If you take freshly made wine and pour it into an old, worn, brittle wineskin, you're in for a leaky surprise. It won't be long, thanks to the fermentation process, before chemical changes in the wine will cause the bag to stretch like a balloon and finally burst.

The old, traditional skin of Judaism was simply too brittle for the new wine of God's kingdom that Jesus was offering. Judaism had become so inflexible that it was not a supple enough womb to give birth to this new era of God's grace. And so attached were the Jews to the wineskins of tradition that they actually preferred their stiff, empty wineskins to the full, festive truth of the gospel.

New-Wine Truths for the Twentieth-Century

Two significant applications jump out of the parable and hurdle the centuries. First: *Our God is a God of freshness and change*. Yet He Himself doesn't change (Heb. 13:8). His character is fixed, but His action is fluid—like a river flowing from a rock. Winding circuitously, the works of God wash freshly over both Testaments.

The Old Testament speaks of a new song . . . a new heart . . . a new spirit . . . a new covenant. The New Testament speaks of a new birth . . . a new creature . . . a new commandment . . . a new heaven and a new earth. The Bible's last reference to *new* is found in Revelation 21:5, where the Lord says that He's "making all things new."

But traditionalism tends to resist the new and retreat to the old. Remember the bronze serpent God told Moses to hold up in the wilderness? It provided healing for those who were dying from snakebites (see Num. 21:8–9). For years the Israelites dragged that serpent around and revered it as a god. For years . . . until at last, God broke their tradition.

> [Hezekiah] removed the high places and broke down the sacred pillars and cut down the Asherah. He also broke in pieces the bronze serpent that Moses had made, for until those days the sons of Israel burned incense to it; and it was called Nehushtan. (2 Kings 18:4)

The second significant fact emerging from Luke 5 is this: *New wineskins are essential, not optional.* Every generation has been tempted to restrict God's dealings. Most people are maintainers, not innovators. That's why traditionalism appeals to the majority.

But in each age, new things are wrought by God. And if we're going to accommodate the new, fresh workings of God, then new wineskins are essential.

Is your wine still fresh, or are you living on experiences from a generation ago? Are you tapping into new, bubbling, sparkling wine? Or has your faith grown flat and tasteless . . . lost its effervescence?

And how about the wineskin? Are you still flexible, or has traditionalism given your life a rigid, brittle texture? How open are you to change? How willing are you to risk? How quickly will you strike out in response to a new direction from God?

As we have seen, our God is a God of the new and fresh. Which means that we, too, are to be people of newness and flexibility. As Paul commands in Ephesians 5:1: "Therefore be imitators of God, as beloved children." We mustn't turn our lips, then, from the new wine of excellence to remain at the old wine of traditional mediocrity.

Living Insights — STUDY ONE

By the time Christ appeared on the scene, the religious leaders had so tightly woven their customs into the fabric of Scripture that it was often difficult to extricate the truth of God from the tangle of human tradition.

But Christ cut through that tangle like a machete hacking through a jungle: God isn't interested in clean hands; He's interested in clean hearts (Mark 7:15). He isn't impressed with lip service (v. 6); He's impressed with obedience (vv. 9–13).

How about you? When you go to church, are you more concerned with the condition of your cashmere blazer than the condition of your heart? Are you more careful not to smear your lipstick than someone's reputation through gossip?

Remember, God isn't concerned with outward appearances—He's concerned with the heart (1 Sam. 16:7).

Living Insights — STUDY TWO

From wine and wineskins we gleaned the lessons of freshness and flexibility. Personally speaking, how are you doing in these two areas? Are your thoughts freshened by creativity? Are you flexible enough to be open, mobile, and willing to risk? Use the space provided to do a little assessing.

In what areas are you most open to the new wine of freshness and creativity?

Which areas are the least open? Why?

What can you do to become more receptive to newness?

How about flexibility? Are you open to change and risk? If not, why?

In what areas do you need to become more flexible?

What can you do, starting today, to begin pouring your life into a new wineskin?

Chapter 13

Removing the Blahs from Today

Psalm 90

Greek mythology records a story about a man with a terminal case of the blahs. His name is Sisyphus. Because Sisyphus had angered the gods, they had sentenced him to an eternity of meaningless labor in Hades. Once there, his onerous task was to repeatedly roll a rock up a hill, only to watch it always roll back down.

Homer, in *The Odyssey*, tells the story.

> "And I saw Sisyphus at his endless task raising his prodigious stone with both his hands. With hands and feet he tried to roll it up to the top of the hill, but always, just before he could roll it over on to the other side, its weight would be too much for him, and the pitiless stone would come thundering down again on to the plain. Then he would begin trying to push it up hill again, and the sweat ran off him and the steam rose after him."[1]

How would you like *his* job? Makes your case of the blahs seem like a vacation on the Riviera, doesn't it? If you ever wanted a story on the wearisome routine of a meaningless life, Sisyphus would be the man to interview!

From time to time we all find ourselves pushing boulders uphill, only to have the burdensome things roll back down again . . . and again . . . and again. If we're not careful, we can get trapped in that meaningless valley, pushing monotonous boulders day in and day out. And before we know it, our lives add up to a lot of sweat and toil and monotony—with meaning evaporating like the steam from Sisyphus' back.

Our psalm for today will take us out of that valley and up to the peaks, opening our eyes to vistas we never knew existed.

1. Homer, *The Odyssey*, in vol. 4 of *Great Books of the Western World*, ed. Robert Maynard Hutchins (Chicago, Ill.: Encyclopaedia Britannica, 1952), p. 248.

Surveying the Psalm

Before we scan the exegetical horizon of Psalm 90, let's focus our binoculars on a few introductory matters.

The Writer

The psalm's superscription reads "A Prayer of Moses the man of God." This is the only psalm attributed to Moses—a man whose life had great meaning but also great periods of monotony. From age forty to age eighty, Moses tended sheep in a desert. Try to imagine the monotony, listening to the same blah baas for forty years! The next forty he spent wandering in the wilderness with a larger, more headstrong flock—the nation of Israel. Wandering in circles year after year . . . the same terrain . . . the same old food . . . the same stubborn people.

His Style

The psalm takes the form of a prayer, with Moses addressing God directly and personally throughout. It begins on a high note, strikes somber chords in the middle stanzas, and then crescendos in an optimistic appeal to God.

An Outline

The psalm begins with a strong emphasis on God in verses 1–2. With verse 3, the emphasis changes to humanity. The final verse brings the psalm full circle to "the Lord our God." Here we are reminded that God's favor in confirming our life and labor is the answer to our drudgery and doldrums. With this God/man/God structure, the psalm pictures the wheat and chaff of humanity held in the tender, cupped hands of the Almighty.

Breaking the Spell

Frequently, our boredom and blahs begin when we fall under monotony's spell. In this quasi-hypnotic state, we experience a spiritual vertigo that blurs everything. If we're not alert, we can be lulled into a stupor of suspended animation, and one day we'll awake to find ourselves yawning in the land of mediocrity. To avoid this, we need to select a reference point and fix our eyes on it until we regain our spiritual balance.

The Right Reference Point

Notice how Moses establishes the right reference point in the first verse: "Lord, Thou hast been our dwelling place in all generations." Philosophers from Plato to Sartre have wrestled with the dilemma of meaning in the universe and have concluded: "A finite point has no meaning unless it has an infinite reference point."[2] For Moses, that infinite reference point was God.

The Right Perspective

Not only is the Lord "the God who is there,"[3] He is the God who is eternal. Eternity is the substance of life's shadows, and if we are to see our own lives in the right perspective, we must see them, as Moses saw his, in light of eternity.

> Before the mountains were born,
> Or Thou didst give birth to the earth and the world,
> Even from everlasting to everlasting, Thou art God.
> (v. 2)

Probing the Soul

As we probe our souls during times of such philosophical wrestlings, three thoughts generally come to mind.

My Life Is So Short

Moses begins his lament about life's brevity with an allusion to the curse that came from the Fall (Gen. 3:19).

> Thou dost turn man back into dust,
> And dost say, "Return, O children of men."
> For a thousand years in Thy sight
> Are like yesterday when it passes by,
> Or as a watch in the night.
> Thou has swept them away like a flood, they fall
> asleep;
> In the morning they are like grass which sprouts
> anew.

2. Francis A. Schaeffer, *The Church at the End of the 20th Century* (Downers Grove, Ill.: InterVarsity Press, 1970), p. 10.

3. Francis A. Schaeffer, *The God Who Is There* (Chicago, Ill.: InterVarsity Press, 1968).

In the morning it flourishes, and sprouts anew;
Toward evening it fades, and withers away.
(Ps. 90:3–6)

Notice the vivid word pictures: "yesterday" . . . a brief "watch in the night"[4] . . . "a flood" . . . "grass." Each image is so ephemeral, like watercolors paling against the canvas of eternity. As James says, we are like "a vapor that appears for a little while and then vanishes away" (4:14b).

My Sins Are So Obvious

A second thought usually lurks just around the corner when the blahs have got us down. We are overwhelmed not only by the brevity of life but also by the blatancy of our sins.

For we have been consumed by Thine anger,
And by Thy wrath we have been dismayed.
Thou hast placed our iniquities before Thee,
Our secret sins in the light of Thy presence.
For all our days have declined in Thy fury;
We have finished our years like a sigh.
As for the days of our life, they contain seventy
  years,
Or if due to strength, eighty years,
Yet their pride is but labor and sorrow;
For soon it is gone and we fly away.
Who understands the power of Thine anger,
And Thy fury, according to the fear that is due Thee?
(Ps. 90:7–11)

Remember the sin that haunted Moses throughout forty years in the desert—the murder of that Egyptian (Exod. 2:11–12)? After many regret-filled years of wandering, carrying the burden of not only his own sins but also those of the nation, no wonder his life winds down with a weary sigh.

My Days Are So Empty

A third feeling often accompanies the blahs—the feeling that

4. In ancient times, the night was divided into three watches lasting four hours each, through which a person might have slept without even being aware of their passing (compare Exod. 14:24 and Judg. 7:19). Later, the night was divided into four watches lasting three hours each.

our lives lack meaning. We know our names are written in God's Book of Life, but we fear that we will be mentioned only in passing, like tombstones inscribed with names but no epitaphs. Moses gives us some valuable advice if we want our lives to be more than just footnotes on the pages of time.

> So teach us to number our days,
> That we may present to Thee a heart of wisdom.
> (Ps. 90:12; see also 39:4)

Philip Bailey developed Moses' thought even further in his insightful poem *Festus*.

> We live in deeds, not in years; in thoughts, not
> breaths;
> In feelings, not in figures on a dial.
> We should count time by heart-throbs. He most lives
> Who thinks most, feels the noblest, acts the best.
> And he whose heart beats quickest lives the longest.
> Life's but a means unto an end; that end—God.[5]

Singing the Song

In numbering his days—learning to live each day to the hilt for eternity—Moses breaks through the blahs. Like the birth of a fresh, new day from the dark womb of night, a song of joy crowns Moses' mental labor.

> Do return, O Lord; how long will it be?
> And be sorry for Thy servants.
> O satisfy us in the morning with Thy loving-
> kindness,
> That we may sing for joy and be glad all our days.
> Make us glad according to the days Thou hast
> afflicted us,
> And the years we have seen evil.
> Let Thy work appear to Thy servants,
> And Thy majesty to their children.
> And let the favor of the Lord our God be upon us;
> And do confirm for us the work of our hands;

5. Philip James Bailey, *Festus*, as quoted in *Handbook of Preaching Resources from Literature*, ed. James D. Robertson (Grand Rapids, Mich.: Baker Book House, 1972), p. 111.

Yes, confirm the work of our hands. (90:13–17)

In this psalm, Moses has written a lot about time and eternity and God's anger and His favor, subjects quite familiar to another psalmist—David.

Sing praise to the Lord, you His godly ones,
And give thanks to His holy name.
For His anger is but for a moment,
His favor is for a lifetime;
Weeping may last for the night,
But a shout of joy comes in the morning. (30:4–5)

If you've been singing the blues about life, maybe it's time to change that old, tired tune. Why don't you sing a new song to the Lord . . . even if you have to sing it in the rain!

Try singing a song like Moses'—a song of consecration that will help you wisely number your days according to the rhythm of eternity. Try taking to heart the words of the hymn "Take My Life and Let It Be," and sing them to the Lord.

Take my life and let it be
Consecrated, Lord, to Thee;
Take my moments and my days,
Let them flow in ceaseless praise.

Take my hands and let them move
At the impulse of Thy love;
Take my feet and let them be
Swift and beautiful for Thee.

Take my voice and let me sing
Always, only, for my King;
Take my lips and let them be
Filled with messages from Thee.

Take my silver and my gold,
Not a mite would I withhold;
Take my intellect and use
Ev'ry pow'r as Thou shalt choose.

Take my will and make it Thine,
It shall be no longer mine;
Take my heart, it is Thine own,
It shall be Thy royal throne.

Take my love, my Lord, I pour
At Thy feet its treasure store;
Take myself, and I will be
Ever, only, all, for Thee.[6]

Living Insights STUDY ONE

Boredom usually results when we feel that what we're doing isn't meaningful. One way we can reconnect with meaning and purpose is to remember who we're living and working for—our Lord who has been a "dwelling place in all generations . . . from everlasting to everlasting" (Ps. 90:1, 2b).

Psalm 90 gives us a rich portrait of our heavenly "boss." Read this psalm's seventeen verses again, and jot down Moses' descriptions of God.

Now, take a look at verse 17:

> And let the favor of the Lord our God be upon us;
> And do confirm for us the work of our hands;
> Yes, confirm the work of our hands.

This word *confirm* can also be rendered "give permanence to." In other words, Moses is saying, "Make what I do with my life last, Lord. Help me see the significance of it in light of Your plan." How can this verse, coupled with the descriptions of God you found, propel you out of monotony's meaningless blahs?

6. Frances R. Havergal, "Take My Life and Let It Be," in *The Lutheran Hymnal* (St. Louis, Mo.: Concordia Publishing House, 1941), no. 400.

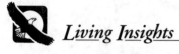

Living Insights STUDY TWO

Any mother with preschoolers or summer vacationers knows the endless question: "Mom, what can I do now?" Boredom, monotony, weary routine . . . sameness lulls us all, adult and child alike, into lethargy. Well, splash some water in your face, because we're going to launch an all-out attack on dullness! Answer the following questions to discover how you can defeat monotony.

What circumstances typically cause you to feel bored?

1. ____________________

2. ____________________

3. ____________________

Is it possible for you to change these circumstances? If so, how will you start?

1. ____________________

____

2. ____________________

____

3. ____________________

____

Whether change is possible or not, how do you think God can use these circumstances to give you added maturity?

1. ____________________

____

2. ____________________

____

3. ____________________

____

Chapter 14

BECOMING A MODEL OF UNSELFISHNESS

Selected Scriptures

Ebenezer Scrooge. The very name sounds stingy, doesn't it? Charles Dickens, in his classic *A Christmas Carol*, describes Scrooge as "hard and sharp as flint, from which no steel had ever struck out generous fire."[1]

Christmas Eve created for Scrooge a begrudged opportunity to show generosity toward one of his employees.

> "You'll want all day to-morrow, I suppose?" said Scrooge.
>
> "If quite convenient, sir."
>
> "It's not convenient," said Scrooge, "and it's not fair. If I was to stop half-a-crown for it, you'd think yourself ill used, I'll be bound?"
>
> The clerk smiled faintly.
>
> "And yet," said Scrooge, "you don't think *me* ill used, when I pay a day's wages for no work."
>
> The clerk observed that it was only once a year.
>
> "A poor excuse for picking a man's pocket every twenty-fifth of December!" said Scrooge, buttoning his great-coat to the chin. "But I suppose you must have the whole day. Be here all the earlier next morning!"
>
> The clerk promised that he would; and Scrooge walked out with a growl.[2]

Hardly a model of joyful generosity! Yet, in exaggerated form, Scrooge does model the attitude many people today have toward giving.

In this study, we will explore what it takes to break that mold and become a true model of joyful generosity instead.

1. Charles Dickens, *A Christmas Carol* (New York, N.Y.: Dial Books, 1983), p. 12.

2. Dickens, *A Christmas Carol*, pp. 21–22.

Mandate for Generosity

Right behind the gold medal of love shines the silver medal of joy (Gal. 5:22). And, like a medal, joy's reflection can hardly be hidden. Proverbs tells us: "A joyful heart makes a cheerful face" (15:13; compare v. 15; 17:22). Just as joy is reflected in our faces, it should also be reflected in our giving. The apostle Paul makes a profound statement to this effect in his second letter to the Corinthians.

> Now this I say, he who sows sparingly shall also reap sparingly; and he who sows bountifully shall also reap bountifully. Let each one do just as he has purposed in his heart; not grudgingly or under compulsion; for God loves a cheerful giver. (9:6–7)

In the Greek text, *cheerful* is the first word in the sentence, thus establishing its emphasis in the author's mind. It comes from the Greek word *hilaros*, from which we get our word *hilarious*. God prizes the hilarious giver—not the grumpy giver. It's not a matter of laughing all the way to the bank, but of laughing all the way to benevolence.

Models of Generosity

Negative models like Scrooge are not enough to repel us from selfishness. We also need positive models to attract us to generosity.

From the Old Testament

We see a classic example of joyful generosity during the Israelites' sojourn in the wilderness. Here God gave them an architectural blueprint for a portable worship center and a pattern for the priestly garments and articles of worship (Exod. 25–31). In Exodus 35:4–19, Moses revealed God's fund-raising plan for the proposed tabernacle—the contributions of the people! The Israelites' response to this request was especially heartwarming because it came not from human coercion but from divine coaxing.

> Then all the congregation of the sons of Israel departed from Moses' presence. And everyone whose heart stirred him and everyone whose spirit moved him came and brought the Lord's contribution for the work of the tent of meeting and for all its service and for the holy garments. Then all whose hearts

> moved them, both men and women, came and brought brooches and earrings and signet rings and bracelets, all articles of gold; so did every man who presented an offering of gold to the Lord. And every man, who had in his possession blue and purple and scarlet material and fine linen and goats' hair and rams' skins dyed red and porpoise skins, brought them. Everyone who could make a contribution of silver and bronze brought the Lord's contribution; and every man, who had in his possession acacia wood for any work of the service, brought it. And all the skilled women spun with their hands, and brought what they had spun, in blue and purple and scarlet material and in fine linen. And all the women whose heart stirred with a skill spun the goats' hair. And the rulers brought the onyx stones and the stones for setting for the ephod and for the breastpiece; and the spice and the oil for the light and for the anointing oil and for the fragrant incense. The Israelites, all the men and women, whose heart moved them to bring material for all the work, which the Lord had commanded through Moses to be done, brought a freewill offering to the Lord. (vv. 20–29)

The Spirit of God moved among the people in a mighty way. In a broad, sweeping gesture of generosity, the nation united around the common cause of constructing for God a dwelling place in their midst. So willing were the people to give of their resources that Moses finally had to stop the flood of offerings (36:2–7). What an incredible model of hilarious generosity![3]

From the New Testament

Crossing the Old Testament's literary border into the pages of the New, we tiptoe into a reverent setting where the wise men are demonstrating joyful giving as they worship young Jesus.

> And when they saw the star, they rejoiced exceedingly with great joy. And they came into the house

3. Another impressive Old Testament model can be found in the rebuilding of Jerusalem's walls during the time of Nehemiah (Neh. 2:17–18; 4:6; 6:15–16).

> and saw the Child with Mary His mother; and they fell down and worshiped Him; and opening their treasures they presented to Him gifts of gold and frankincense and myrrh. (Matt. 2:10–11)

What characterized their attitudes? Joy. Exceedingly great joy. The result? Generosity. Extravagant generosity. Joy's effervescence bubbles into all areas of our lives, and when it touches our wallets, it overflows in extravagance.

How extravagant is your giving? Does the clattering of collection plates cause you to cringe in your padded pew? Do your George Washingtons squint painfully when exposed to the light of day? If so, maybe you have more of a bah-humbug attitude than one of festive Christmas joy. The problem may be that rather than the Savior sitting on the throne of your life, there crouches the silhouette of Scrooge, hoarding your money . . . at your own expense.

Methods for Motivating Generosity

Turning from biblical models of magnanimity, let's give our attention to three methods for bringing joy and generosity back into our lives.

Reflect on God's Gifts to You

In Psalm 103, David shows us how to meditate on God's blessings.

> Bless the Lord, O my soul;
> And all that is within me, bless His holy name.
> Bless the Lord, O my soul,
> And forget none of His benefits;
> Who pardons all your iniquities;
> Who heals all your diseases;
> Who redeems your life from the pit;
> Who crowns you with lovingkindness and compassion;
> Who satisfies your years with good things,
> So that your youth is renewed like the eagle.
> (vv. 1–5)

What iniquities of yours has God pardoned? From what diseases has He healed you? From what pit has He rescued you? How has He bestowed His love and kindness on you? All that we have are gifts from God—eyesight . . . memory . . . skill . . . money . . . family—gifts sourced in the hilarious generosity of God.

Remind Yourself of His Promises regarding Generosity

If we sow bountifully, we shall reap bountifully (2 Cor. 9:6b).

> The generous man will be prosperous,
> And he who waters will himself be watered.
> (Prov. 11:25)
>
> "Give, and it will be given to you; good measure, pressed down, shaken together, running over, they will pour into your lap. For by your standard of measure it will be measured to you in return." (Luke 6:38)

Examine Your Heart

Audit the ledger of your heart's motivations. Here are a couple of questions to get you started: Am I giving out of guilt or out of joy? Am I trying to please my peers as they look over my shoulder, or am I trying to please God, who sees in secret?

A Majestic Model of Generosity

Sometimes we tend to picture God as a miserly old man, clutching His wealth of blessings with a tight fist. Consequently, we pray as though we're pleading for God to pry those blessings loose. Nothing could be further from the truth. John 3:16 cameos a more accurate image of God.

For God	the greatest giver
so loved	the greatest motive
the world	the greatest need
that He gave	the greatest act
His only begotten Son	the greatest gift
that whoever	the greatest invitation
believes in Him	the greatest opportunity
should not perish	the greatest deliverance
but have eternal life	the greatest joy

A Concluding Word

Despite his miserly beginnings, Ebenezer Scrooge had a magnanimous ending. A changed man by virtue of several telling encounters, he came on Christmas Day to the home of his employee

Bob Cratchit . . . to make amends.

> "A merry Christmas, Bob!" said Scrooge, with an earnestness that could not be mistaken, as he clapped him on the back. "A merrier Christmas, Bob, my good fellow, than I have given you, for many a year! I'll raise your salary, and endeavour to assist your struggling family. . . ."
>
> . . . Scrooge was better than his word. He did it all, and infinitely more. . . . He became as good a friend, as good a master, and as good a man, as the good old city knew; . . . and it was always said of him, that he knew how to keep Christmas well.[4]

If Dickens could change Scrooge, certainly Jesus—the author of our faith—can change the most begrudging of us into joyful, hilarious givers.

Living Insights STUDY ONE

Jesus told His disciples as He sent them on their first missionary journey: "Freely you received, freely give" (Matt. 10:8b). Could it be that we give grudgingly, like Scrooge, because we've never really come to grips with grace? Could it be that we have difficulty giving freely because we have never received freely?

Have you accepted God's free gift of salvation through Jesus Christ?

If not, you can do that right now, right where you are. You don't need special training and you don't have to be in a special holy place. You can just pray, telling Him you want John 3:16, which we outlined toward the end of our study, to be true of you and your life. He is nearer than you know, and He longs to welcome you into His kingdom.[5]

4. Dickens, *A Christmas Carol*, pp. 126–27.

5. If you do choose to give your heart to Christ, or if you have questions you need answered first, our counselors at Insight for Living would be very glad to hear from you. Our address is Insight for Living, Post Office Box 69000, Anaheim, CA 92817-0900.

If Christ already is your Savior, do you still have difficulty receiving His gifts? Do you feel you have to work your way into His good graces? What is your perception of God's attitude toward you?

To counter any miserly pictures of Him that you may be carrying around in your mind, spend some time gazing at the portraits His Word has provided for us. What impact does each of the following passages have on you?

Romans 8:15–16, 31–32

Galatians 3:2–3; 5:1

Ephesians 1:3–8a

Ephesians 2:1–10

Ephesians 2:17–19

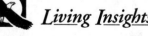

Living Insights STUDY TWO

Perhaps another reason we don't freely give what we have freely received is that we take all that we get for granted—to the point that sometimes we don't even see it anymore. Is this true of you? To clear your vision, blink in a few clear, warm drops of gratefulness.

Using Psalm 103 as your model, write down everything in your life you can be thankful for. Big or little; it doesn't matter. What matters is opening the eyes of your heart "to the riches of His grace, which He lavished upon us" (Eph. 1:7b–8a).

What I Have to Be Grateful For

Part Four

Resisting Mediocrity Includes Standing Courageously

Chapter 15

STANDING ALONE WHEN OUTNUMBERED

Romans 12:1–2; Deuteronomy 6:10–15

Remember the Alamo!" This cry has immortalized that famous Texas battle in our memories.

The siege on the San Antonio mission lasted from February 23 to March 6, 1836. Under General Santa Anna, 5,000 Mexican troops surrounded the Alamo and attacked it for thirteen days. Outnumbered almost 30 to 1, the Texas volunteers stood alone and fought valiantly. One by one, their ranks were thinned by the enemy's bullets and cannonballs. As the battle climaxed with a massive attack over the mission walls, all 182 men were killed.

The volunteers' strategy had been to delay the Mexican forces long enough for the Texas settlers to organize an army. And their supreme sacrifice did just that. A short time later, Texas troops under General Sam Houston mounted a surprise attack at San Jacinto, captured Santa Anna, and secured independence for Texas.[1]

Even though the battle of the Alamo was lost, the war for Texas independence was won—all because of a band of dedicated men who were not afraid to stand alone when outnumbered.

Standing Alone against the World

Standing alone is never easy. Yet we have the assurance that "if God is for us, who is against us?" (Rom. 8:31b). God plus one always equals a majority; and, though we may lose some of the battles in this life, we know that the war will ultimately be won in eternity. The world may storm our walls, but it can't conquer our souls.

The Exhortation

In Romans 12:1–2, Paul urgently pleads with believers to break away from the herd instinct—to stand alone with God instead of following the majority.

> I urge you therefore, brethren, by the mercies of

1. Lon Tinkle, *The Alamo* (New York, N.Y.: McGraw-Hill Book Co., 1958).

> God, to present your bodies a living and holy sacrifice, acceptable to God, which is your spiritual service of worship. And do not be conformed to this world, but be transformed by the renewing of your mind, that you may prove what the will of God is, that which is good and acceptable and perfect.

Note that the passage is not referring to the salvation of the unsaved—"brethren"; nor is it suggesting an optional course of action—"I urge you"; nor is it implying that it will be easy—"sacrifice." Instead, standing alone will take all that we have, our inner selves as well as our physical bodies, which is found in the word "present." As Donald Grey Barnhouse notes in his commentary on Romans, "There is both the body to be presented and the self that does the presenting."[2]

Putting each of these pieces together, Barnhouse remarks on this passage:

> Not conformed, but transformed . . . this is the life of the true believer in Christ. The first of these two words, *conformed*, is the translation of a Greek word in the New Testament and it means that we are not to go along with the world's schemes. The second of these words, *transformed*, is a Greek word which means a very radical change from one nature and life to another. It is the word *metamorphoomai* which has given us our word *metamorphosis*. When a tadpole is changed into a frog or when a grub becomes a butterfly, we speak of it as metamorphosis. There has been a marked and more or less abrupt change in the form and structure of the creature.[3]

The Explanation

For the believer, that change isn't cosmetic surgery but radical reconstruction—from a human shaped by the world to one being

2. Donald Grey Barnhouse, *God's Discipline*, in *Expositions of Bible Doctrines Taking the Epistle to the Romans as a Point of Departure*, vol. 4 (1964; reprint, Grand Rapids, Mich.: William B. Eerdmans Publishing Co., 1988), p. 10.

3. Barnhouse, *God's Discipline*, p. 27.

conformed to God's image, which is Jesus Christ (see Rom. 8:29; 1 John 3:2). In other words, consecrating our lives to Christ involves more than simply shedding our skin like a snake. It involves our complete metamorphosis.

Metamorphosis is seen most dramatically and beautifully in butterflies, where the larval stage differs greatly from the adult. This transformation occurs during the inactive pupal stage, in which the organs and tissues break down into liquid and are reorganized into an adult structure.

In human terms, we can sometimes grovel in the world's dirt, worming around in our little vermicular routines. But if we want more than just a seasonal changing of skins, if God is going to truly transform our lives, we'll have to lie down on the altar. Because before God can ever give us wings, He must dissolve our old self and restructure it according to His design.

Sizing Up the World's Mold

The Phillips translation of Romans 12:2 reads: "Don't let the world around you squeeze you into its own mould." The contours of the world's mold flow along the lines of *fortune*—money and materialism; *fame*—popularity and acceptance; *power*—influence and control; and *pleasure*—sensual desires.

If our inner convictions lie lumped in a pliable, amorphous mass, we'll be shaped by our peers instead of by God. "Do not be deceived," Paul warns in 1 Corinthians 15:33, "Bad company corrupts good morals." The wisdom of Solomon reflects the same conclusion concerning the pervasive influence of our associates:

> He who walks with wise men will be wise,
> But the companion of fools will suffer harm.
> (Prov. 13:20)

Stampeded by the Herd

If you're following the herd, before you know it, you may find yourself caught up in a stampede, running with the crowd at breakneck speed. And if you're not careful, you may just find yourself plunging headlong off the side of a moral cliff. Moses warned the Israelites of just such a peril as they were about to enter the Promised Land, where they would encounter a wild herd of Canaanites.

> "Then it shall come about when the Lord your

> God brings you into the land which He swore to your fathers, Abraham, Isaac and Jacob, to give you, great and splendid cities which you did not build, and houses full of all good things which you did not fill, and hewn cisterns which you did not dig, vineyards and olive trees which you did not plant, and you shall eat and be satisfied, then watch yourself, lest you forget the Lord who brought you from the land of Egypt, out of the house of slavery. You shall fear only the Lord your God; and you shall worship Him, and swear by His name. You shall not follow other gods, any of the gods of the peoples who surround you, for the Lord your God in the midst of you is a jealous God; otherwise the anger of the Lord your God will be kindled against you, and He will wipe you off the face of the earth." (Deut. 6:10–15)

Don't think for a moment that God doesn't care about the conduct of His children. Like a protective parent, He watches for dangers to which we are oblivious. How easy it would be for the Israelites to follow the wrong role models. How easy it would be to forget who gave them the roof over their heads, the food on their plates, and the keys to their camels. Between the lines, Moses urges the adolescent nation to stand alone . . . to not yield to peer pressure . . . to not follow the pack.

Standing against the Herd

Four principles emerge from this passage: (1) getting something for nothing breeds irresponsibility; (2) this, then, creates a careless attitude; (3) this, in turn, can lead to a loss of standards; (4) that lack of standards prompts insecurity—which drives us into the "safety" of conformity.

No illustration of this stands out so clearly as the generation that entered the Promised Land. They forgot their Father and succumbed to the pressure of their peers.

How do we keep from forgetting God when the pressure of the world squeezes hard against our lives? In Deuteronomy 6:4–9, Moses gave the Israelites a string to tie around their mental fingers.

> "Hear, O Israel! The Lord is our God, the Lord is one! And you shall love the Lord your God with

> all your heart and with all your soul and with all your might. And these words, which I am commanding you today, shall be on your heart; and you shall teach them diligently to your sons and shall talk of them when you sit in your house and when you walk by the way and when you lie down and when you rise up. And you shall bind them as a sign on your hand and they shall be as frontals on your forehead. And you shall write them on the doorposts of your house and on your gates."

Moses' advice is just as timely today. If we will take it to heart, it will help us remember God in our daily lives so that we will be able to stand alone—even when outnumbered by a herd of Canaanites!

Living Insights STUDY ONE

Dr. James Dobson, in his excellent book *Hide or Seek*, warns that adolescents are most vulnerable to getting squeezed into the world's mold because of peer pressure.

> The pressure to follow the whims of the group (called the herd instinct) is never so great as it is during the adolescent years. This drive may be all-consuming to a teen-ager when *any* deviation from the "in" behavior is a serious breach of etiquette. And there is tyranny in this pressure. . . . Each teen-ager knows that safety from ridicule can only be found by remaining precisely on the chalk line of prevailing opinion.[4]

To help keep your kids walking in the light instead of being stampeded into the world's darkness, you need to be aware of what is influencing their lives. The following questions can help get you started.

With what kinds of friends do your children surround themselves?

---

4. James Dobson, *Hide or Seek*, rev. ed. (Old Tappan, N.J.: Fleming H. Revell Co., 1979), p. 126.

What kinds of books are they reading?

What kinds of television shows and movies and music do they take in?

These will all play a part in molding their lives; for better or for worse, they will leave their imprint. What specific imprints are they leaving in your children's lives?

If you like what you see, let your kids know! If you don't like what's there, though, rather than flat-out condemning it, think of some positive steps you can take to gently lead your children back to Christ's transforming presence. We'll list a few ideas to help get you started.

Learn what needs of your child's are being met through his or her friends.

Share with your child the books and movies that have impacted your life.

Research the life of a classical music composer together—then go to a concert.

Find a Christian equivalent of the style of music your child likes.

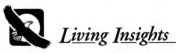

Living Insights STUDY TWO

You've looked at your children; now it's time to look at yourself. Have you ever seriously considered how the world subtly squeezes you into its mold? Let's apply those questions we asked about your children to you. How is your life being impacted by each area?

With what kinds of friends do you surround yourself? Are they more conforming or transforming?

What kinds of books are you reading? What sort of an impact are they having?

What kinds of television shows and movies and music do you take in? What messages are they communicating? How are they affecting your thinking?

If any of these areas are buzzing you like a cattle prod, trying to get you to stop thinking for yourself and move along with the herd, what do you need to change to bolster your strength to stand alone?

Chapter 16

Standing Tall When Tested

Deuteronomy 6:3–9, 12; Judges 3:1–7

"Close your books. Put away your notes. Take out a pencil and a clean sheet of notebook paper . . . pop quiz!"

Bring back memories? Bad memories, most likely. Can you still feel a tremor of low-voltage terror at the mention of those words? Can you still hear your groans echo those of the rest of the class?

Pop quiz—probably the two words the average student fears most. Yet that method of testing is one of the most effective means teachers have of finding out exactly what their students know. God tests us in a similar way, but not to see what's in our brains . . . to see what's in our hearts.

In Genesis, God tested Abraham's faith with a pop quiz involving Isaac (22:1–19). In Deuteronomy, God handed Israel a forty-year wilderness quiz, testing them to find out what was in their hearts (8:2). And in Judges, after the Israelites graduated from the wilderness and were promoted into the Promised Land, God gave them another test.

Would they slump at their desks and fail the exam, or would they stand tall when tested?

The Test

As we saw in our previous chapter, Moses had prepared the Israelites for this quiz with a series of lectures recorded in Deuteronomy and handed down through the generations.

> "O Israel, you should listen and be careful to do it, that it may be well with you and that you may multiply greatly, just as the Lord, the God of your fathers, has promised you, in a land flowing with milk and honey.
>
> "Hear, O Israel! The Lord is our God, the Lord is one! And you shall love the Lord your God with all your heart and with all your soul and with all your might. And these words, which I am commanding

> you today, shall be on your heart; and you shall teach them diligently to your sons and shall talk of them when you sit in your house and when you walk by the way and when you lie down and when you rise up. And you shall bind them as a sign on your hand and they shall be as frontals on your forehead. And you shall write them on the doorposts of your house and on your gates.
>
> "Then it shall come about when the Lord your God brings you into the land which He swore to your fathers, . . . then watch yourself, lest you forget the Lord who brought you from the land of Egypt, out of the house of slavery. You shall fear only the Lord your God; and you shall worship Him, and swear by His name. You shall not follow other gods, any of the gods of the peoples who surround you, for the Lord your God in the midst of you is a jealous God; otherwise the anger of the Lord your God will be kindled against you, and He will wipe you off the face of the earth." (6:3–10a, 12–15)

Once they entered the Promised Land, it was time to close the books, put away the notes, take out pencil and paper, and start the new test. Referring to the nations that surrounded Israel, Judges 3:4 states the test's educational objectives:

> And they were for testing Israel, to find out if they would obey the commandments of the Lord, which He had commanded their fathers through Moses.

Their Situation

First, *the Israelites were alone and uncertain*. Like timid freshmen on the first day of high school, they wandered around the halls, sizing up their situation. And it didn't look good.

> Now it came about after the death of Joshua that the sons of Israel inquired of the Lord, saying, "Who shall go up first for us against the Canaanites, to fight against them?" (1:1)

Second, *they were inexperienced and vulnerable*. The generation who now found themselves in the Promised Land apparently had failed to get their parents' notes from Moses' lectures.

> And all that generation also were gathered to their fathers; and there arose another generation after them who did not know the Lord, nor yet the work which He had done for Israel. (2:10)

Something vital is lost when a nation becomes severed from its historical and spiritual roots. Its strength of character is sapped. Its will to fight to preserve its heritage withers.

Third, *they were surrounded and outnumbered.*

> Now these are the nations which the Lord left, to test Israel by them . . . : the five lords of the Philistines and all the Canaanites and the Sidonians and the Hivites who lived in Mount Lebanon, from Mount Baal-hermon as far as Lebo-hamath. (3:1a, 3)

Archaeology has uncovered something about the culture that surrounded the Israelites at the time. The Ugaritic epic literature of the ancient Semites reveals the depth of depravity that characterized the Canaanite religion in their worship of numerous gods, including El, Baal, Anath, Astarte, and Asherah. "The brutality, lust and abandon of Canaanite mythology is far worse than elsewhere in the Near East at the time."[1] Hebrew scholar Leah Bronner notes:

> The gods themselves indulge in all pleasures, eating, drinking, and lovemaking, and perpetrate some of the most abominable deeds. They lived immoral lives, hated, warred, and killed often only for fun. . . . It is these lascivious practices, such as bestiality, temple prostitution, and child sacrifice, that are associated with Baal, which evoked the bitter invective of the prophets against the sensual Canaanite cult.[2]

Things don't look good for the freshman class at Canaanite High. They are alone and uncertain, inexperienced and vulnerable, surrounded and outnumbered.

1. Merrill F. Unger, *Archaeology and the Old Testament* (Grand Rapids, Mich.: Zondervan Publishing House, 1954), p. 175.

2. Leah Bronner, *Biblical Personalities and Archaeology* (Jerusalem, Israel: Keter Publishing House Jerusalem, 1974), p. 84.

Have you ever felt like these second-generation Israelites? You may not benefit much from last-minute cramming for the test you're taking now, but it wouldn't hurt to crack open the Book and review God's educational objectives for such testing:

> Consider it all joy, my brethren, when you encounter various trials, knowing that the testing of your faith produces endurance. And let endurance have its perfect result, that you may be perfect and complete, lacking in nothing. (James 1:2–4)

Their Reaction

The first thing we notice about the Israelites' reaction to the test is *a lack of total obedience*. The Lord had issued His battle strategy in Deuteronomy 7:1–2:

> "When the Lord your God shall bring you into the land where you are entering to possess it, and shall clear away many nations before you, . . . then you shall utterly destroy them. You shall make no covenant with them and show no favor to them."

However, as the grade book of Judges 1:19 records, the class fell short of a perfect score.

> Now the Lord was with Judah, and they took possession of the hill country; but they could not drive out the inhabitants of the valley.

And the test scores only got worse—

> But the sons of Benjamin did not drive out the Jebusites who lived in Jerusalem; so the Jebusites have lived with the sons of Benjamin in Jerusalem to this day. (v. 21)

And worse—

> But Manasseh did not take possession of Beth-shean and its villages, or Taanach and its villages, or the inhabitants of Dor and its villages, or the inhabitants of Ibleam and its villages, or the inhabitants of Megiddo and its villages; so the Canaanites persisted in living in that land. (v. 27)

And worse—

> Naphtali did not drive out the inhabitants of Beth-shemesh, or the inhabitants of Beth-anath, but lived among the Canaanites, the inhabitants of the land; and the inhabitants of Beth-shemesh and Beth-anath became forced labor for them. (v. 33)

The second thing we notice about the reaction of Israel is that they suffered *a loss of spiritual distinction*. Because they lacked total obedience—deciding to coexist with the Canaanites instead of obliterating them from the land—the Israelites compromised their way to spiritual infidelity.

> Then the sons of Israel did evil in the sight of the Lord, and served the Baals, and they forsook the Lord, the God of their fathers, who had brought them out of the land of Egypt, and followed other gods from among the gods of the peoples who were around them, and bowed themselves down to them; thus they provoked the Lord to anger. (2:11–12)

Finally, there was *a loosening of marital restrictions*.

> And the sons of Israel lived among the Canaanites, the Hittites, the Amorites, the Perizzites, the Hivites, and the Jebusites; and they took their daughters for themselves as wives, and gave their own daughters to their sons, and served their gods. (3:5–6)

The nation drifted into the shallow, precarious harbor of intermarriage between themselves and the Canaanites—a union explicitly forbidden by God (Deut. 7:3–4). And sure enough, before long, Israel was on the rocks in their relationship with the Lord.

> And the sons of Israel did what was evil in the sight of the Lord, and forgot the Lord their God, and served the Baals and the Asheroth. (Judg. 3:7)

The Homework

To keep ourselves from failing the same test, a little homework is in order. Take notes and file away the following principles.

First, *standing tall starts with the way we think*. It involves a mindset: the way we think about God, ourselves, and others. And our mental lenses color the way we view the rest of life—school, dating, marriage, business, family.

Second, *standing tall calls for strong discipline*. This involves our will—disciplining our eyes, hands, feet, and tongue. Keeping a short leash on the areas where we are prone to wander goes a long way in keeping us on the straight-and-narrow path of obedience.

Third, *standing tall limits our choice of personal friends*. Hang around the wrong crowd in the halls and you'll be sitting in the back of the class, staying after school, and maybe flunking out of life altogether. Remember Proverbs 13:20:

> He who walks with wise men will be wise,
> But the companion of fools will suffer harm.

Not bad advice. Particularly if you want to graduate from life with honors!

Living Insights — STUDY ONE

Whether the second generation cut class or their parents dropped the ball tutoring them (compare Deut. 6:4–9), the results are clear—the new generation of Israelites was not ready for the test God had prepared.

Home holds the undergraduate degree that is the prerequisite for the Master's program of life. As parents, how well are you preparing your children for the pop quizzes and midterms in God's curriculum?

Perhaps a good way to begin would be to share your spiritual heritage with your child. Do you have a grandfather or a great-great-great uncle who was a preacher? Do you come from a long line of believers who have paid special attention to the way God has worked in their lives? Maybe you are the first in your family to become a Christian. You might have opened the door for the rest of your family to walk through to Jesus Christ. Or maybe all doors were slammed in your face and persecution became your new companion.

Whatever your story, share it with your child. Show them what God has done in your life . . . and can do in theirs.

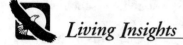

Living Insights STUDY TWO

Well, how is your homework coming? What—you haven't started? Then turn off the television and let's get busy!

Your assignment at the conclusion of our lesson dealt with three "standing tall" statements—principles that call for personalization. Dig right in, then, and think carefully about how you're doing in each area.

- *Standing tall starts with the way we think.* In your business, dating relationships, schooling, marriage, renting arrangements, leadership—does biblical thinking guide your decisions and behavior? Or do you usually follow the world's way? How is your thinking outwardly revealed?

  ___

  ___

  ___

  Of the areas listed above, is there one particular area of struggle for you? What is it, and what are the words your mind uses here?

  ___

  ___

  ___

  With the help of a concordance or topical Bible, find several verses that deal specifically with this area and that have a strong impact on you. Write them on a card, so you can carry your new thoughts with you when you enter your challenging situations.

- *Standing tall calls for strong discipline.* Does your will stand tall like an immovable redwood, or does it bend and snap like a sapling in the strong winds of testing and temptation?

  ___

  ___

What usually pushes you to your breaking point? Peer pressure? Wanting to please others? A desire for pleasure?

How can you apply Solomon's counsel in Proverbs 4:25–27 to those things that compromise your will?

- *Standing tall limits our choice of personal friends*. Whew! This has been a tough bit of homework. Let's end the assignment on a positive note, shall we? Name three friends who help you stand tall, and explain their unique ways of positively impacting you.

1. ____________ ____________________

2. ____________ ____________________

3. ____________ ____________________

Now plan to spend some time with them this week! (You may even be so daring as to tell them about the positive effect they have in your life.)

Chapter 17

STANDING FIRM WHEN DISCOURAGED

Judges 6:1–24, 33–35; 7:2–15; 8:22–23

In the ancient Near East, rainwater was caught and stored in cisterns, or wells. Usually constructed in the shape of a bottle, cisterns had small, circular openings at the top and larger, spherical shapes below the surface of the ground.

Into such a well Jacob's jealous sons threw their brother Joseph, thinking the young boy was doomed to slow starvation (see Gen. 37:18–24). The brothers then sat down to eat, refreshing and nourishing themselves in grassy, sunny comfort, while their brother was crying for mercy in a dark, dank pit.[1]

At some point, we will each experience the rejection, the isolation, the loneliness, the discouragement of the well. Some of us, like Joseph, experience these things through no fault of our own. Others, however, are like the entire nation of Israel in our story today—in a pit of their own making, placed there by the disciplinary hand of God. In Joseph's situation, God used a Midianite caravan to rescue him from the well. For Israel, God used a man named Gideon.

Getting Into the Well of Discouragement

Gideon was a man who stood firm when discouraged. Against his culture, Gideon stood out like a bright star in a moonless night. But before we turn the telescope on his life, let's examine the dark sky of history that presented such a striking contrast.

Israel's Historical State

During Gideon's time, no monarch ruled over Israel. The people had no one to give direction, no one to set the pace, no one to model the truth or give instruction in righteousness. Judges 21:25

1. This part of the account does not mention Joseph's appeals for help, but twenty-one years later the brothers, remorseful at last, recall the incident: "Truly we are guilty concerning our brother, because we saw the distress of his soul when he pleaded with us, yet we would not listen" (Gen. 42:21).

describes the setting: "In those days there was no king in Israel; everyone did what was right in his own eyes." With situation ethics making up the moral climate of the day, it's no wonder that ethical judgments were weighed with a thumb on the scale. Judges 6:1 measures the loss of morality and its consequences:

> Then the sons of Israel did what was evil in the sight of the Lord; and the Lord gave them into the hands of Midian seven years.

The Midianites devastated and demoralized the Israelites, degrading them to such an extent that they were forced to live like animals.

> And the power of Midian prevailed against Israel. Because of Midian the sons of Israel made for themselves the dens which were in the mountains and the caves and the strongholds. For it was when Israel had sown, that the Midianites would come up with the Amalekites and the sons of the east and go against them. So they would camp against them and destroy the produce of the earth as far as Gaza, and leave no sustenance in Israel as well as no sheep, ox, or donkey. For they would come up with their livestock and their tents, they would come in like locusts for number, both they and their camels were innumerable; and they came into the land to devastate it. (vv. 2–5)

Israel's Spiritual State

The spiritual condition of Israel at the time gives life to these words of Jesus: "No one can serve two masters; for either he will hate the one and love the other, or he will hold to one and despise the other" (Matt. 6:24a). Israel initially thought peaceful coexistence was possible between the Lord and the gods of Canaan, but that inevitably led to compromise, and with compromise came a confusion of loyalties. Eventually, Israel's allegiance shifted. Judges 2:12 marks the beginning of this departure.

> And they forsook the Lord, the God of their fathers, who had brought them out of the land of Egypt, and followed other gods from among the gods of the peoples who were around them, and bowed themselves

down to them; thus they provoked the Lord to anger.

The result of God's anger? "Israel was brought very low" (6:6a). So low they had to look up to see the bottom. So low they had nowhere else to look but to God: "and the sons of Israel cried to the Lord" (v. 6b).

Getting Out of the Well of Discouragement

Five principles emerge in the account of Israel's deliverance that can serve as ropes to lift us from the depths of discouragement.

Openly Acknowledge What Caused Your Condition

Through an unnamed prophet, God gave Israel a direct answer regarding what had caused them to fall into the well.

> "'And I said to you, "I am the Lord your God; you shall not fear the gods of the Amorites in whose land you live. But you have not obeyed Me."'" (v. 10)

In a word: disobedience. But in owning up to their sin, the Israelites took the first step toward climbing out of the well. However, not all who stumbled into that well were there because of disobedience. Gideon, for one, had followed the Lord and kept to the straight-and-narrow path of obedience. But doubts arose in his mind when he couldn't reconcile his circumstances with his faith.

> Then Gideon said to [the angel of the Lord], "O my lord, if the Lord is with us, why then has all this happened to us? And where are all His miracles which our fathers told us about, saying, 'Did not the Lord bring us up from Egypt?' But now the Lord has abandoned us and given us into the hand of Midian." (v. 13)

With a mandate of hope, the Lord began to dispel Gideon's doubts and discouragement.[2]

> And the Lord looked at him and said, "Go in this

2. Yet we see in the well-known incident of Gideon's fleece that his doubt was not totally dispelled (Judg. 6:36–40). Like Thomas, he apparently needed some visual form of confirmation of God's word before he could fully believe. So just as Christ did with Thomas, God met Gideon where he was and agreed to answer the request for tangible support.

> your strength and deliver Israel from the hand of Midian. Have I not sent you?" And he said to Him, "O Lord, how shall I deliver Israel? Behold, my family is the least in Manasseh, and I am the youngest in my father's house." But the Lord said to him, "Surely I will be with you, and you shall defeat Midian as one man." (vv. 14–16)

Focus Directly on the Lord, Not on the Odds against You

Responding with faith and commitment, Gideon built an altar to dedicate himself to the task of delivering Israel.

> Then Gideon built an altar there to the Lord and named it The Lord is Peace. To this day it is still in Ophrah of the Abiezrites. (v. 24)

The next time we see Gideon, he is alone, outnumbered, and opposed—in a discouraging situation—but standing firm, nevertheless (vv. 33–35).

Declare Your Allegiance Publicly

When the Spirit of the Lord came upon him, Gideon summoned the troops with a trumpet call (v. 34). God honored his public declaration of allegiance, and the troops rallied behind him and fell in rank. Have you made it known to others where you stand? The trumpet of your testimony must be sounded if you are to gain any degree of victory.

Remember That God Prefers to Work through a Remnant

God does His best work, it seems, when those who serve Him are fewer than those against Him. Note His rationale for paring down the troops to fight the Midianites.

> And the Lord said to Gideon, "The people who are with you are too many for Me to give Midian into their hands, lest Israel become boastful, saying, 'My own power has delivered me.'" (7:2)

Bolt by bolt, God radically cut the fabric of Israel's army, until, at last, only a three-hundred-man swatch remained (vv. 3–8). In His divine stitch work, God prefers working with remnants. The first church was led by a remnant of twelve, and the Reformation was spearheaded by a scrap of pastors. Doubtless, the situation you're in at school, at work, in your neighborhood, renders you a minority also; but remember, that's one of God's favorite ways to work. So be encouraged—you're in good company!

Do Not Accept the Glory after God Uses Your Life

God used Gideon in a miraculous way to deliver Israel from the Midianites (vv. 9–25). Victorious, the Israelites experienced not only peace but prosperity as well. For the first time in years, they had roofs over their heads and food on their plates. To express their gratitude, they offered Gideon the monarchy.

> Then the men of Israel said to Gideon, "Rule over us, both you and your son, also your son's son, for you have delivered us from the hand of Midian." (8:22)

It would have been so easy for the valiant warrior to ride the wave of his military success to the lush shores of fame and fortune. But examine his unselfish response.

> "I will not rule over you, nor shall my son rule over you; the Lord shall rule over you." (v. 23)

A Concluding Application

At any given time, we are choosing to focus on one of four things: our circumstances, others, ourselves, or the Lord.

When outnumbered, Gideon refused to focus on his circumstances. And when victorious against overwhelming odds, he refused to shine the spotlight on himself. Instead, he gave the glory to the Lord.

An eagle's eyes are amazingly keen. On a clear day, an eagle can spot a dead fish floating on the surface of a lake five miles away. That's focus! If we're ever to stand firm in the midst of discouragement, we have to develop spiritual eyesight with similar clarity and concentration—even if we're the only bird in the flock to have it.

Living Insights STUDY ONE

Have you ever known such deep discouragement as the oppressed Israelites? Have you ever felt as if you were dropped into a well of insurmountable circumstances and left there to die? Maybe you're at the bottom of such a well right now.

Rather than have you name it, answer questions about it, and write a mini-essay detailing your action plan to overcome this discouragement, we would humbly and softly suggest something else. Find a quiet, private place, and look up to the Lord, as the Israelites did, and cry out to Him for help.

Unburden your heart to Him, sharing not just the particulars of your circumstances but how desperate, sad, angry, or disheartened you feel. Let His presence and care remind you that you are not alone in this.

> I will lift up my eyes to the mountains;
> From whence shall my help come?
> My help comes from the Lord,
> Who made heaven and earth.
> He will not allow your foot to slip;
> He who keeps you will not slumber.
> Behold, He who keeps Israel
> Will neither slumber nor sleep. (Ps. 121:1–4)

Living Insights STUDY TWO

Gideons are as scarce today as ever, but God still prizes people who stand firmly focused on Him in the face of discouragement. He still looks for people who will "stand in the gap," as He told the prophet Ezekiel,

> "And I searched for a man among them who should build up the wall and stand in the gap before Me for the land, that I should not destroy it; but I found no one." (Ezek. 22:30)

Our world, too, stands perilously close to destruction. Wars sprout and hang on with all the noxious tenacity of weeds. The powerful few feed on the starving many to sate their greed and lust. There's corruption, oppression, pollution, persecution. Global warming could just as well refer to the heating up of hatred and brutal selfishness as much as anything else.

But we don't need to circle the globe to see we're in trouble, do we? The sphere of our own worlds holds enough evidence through the violence, heartbreak, and despair we read about and know firsthand.

Could you be the Gideon—the one to stand in the gap in your family, school, business, neighborhood, city—for whom God searches? What is it that you think God would have you do?

____

____

____

Is there something keeping you from doing that? Some intimidation? Discouragement? What keeps you from being someone who stands firm in the gap?

____

____

____

As Christians, we each have the responsibility and the privilege to do this ministry of standing in the gap—or, in New Testament language, this ministry of reconciliation. As the apostle Paul wrote:

> Now all these things are from God, who reconciled us to Himself through Christ, and gave us the ministry of reconciliation, namely, that God was in Christ reconciling the world to Himself, not counting their trespasses against them, and He has committed to us the word of reconciliation.
>
> Therefore, we are ambassadors for Christ, as though God were entreating through us. (2 Cor. 5:18–20a)

What one thing can you do this week to help bridge the gap between God and someone in your world who needs Him? Pray about this, and when you decide what to do, write it down here as a reminder and an encouragement for the future.

____

____

____

Chapter 18

BOATS, NETS, FISH, AND FAITH

Luke 5:1–11

Grauman's Chinese Theater—probably the most famous motion picture theater in all the world. Ever since May 18, 1927, this renowned Hollywood cinema, now known as Mann's Chinese Theaters, has hosted the film industry's greatest stars in their finest roles.

Since its debut, more than 150 film personalities have embedded their footprints, handprints, signatures, and personal comments in the specially prepared concrete at the theater's entrance. From Abbott and Costello to *Star Wars*' R2-D2 and C-3PO, this concrete has fixed celebrities in its firm, gray memory.

Similarly, there was a place in the memories of the disciples where Jesus made a permanent impression. A place where He put His hands and feet and words in the wet cement of their lives and made an imprint so deep and profound, it would forever mold their lives.

The Setting

The incident began on the damp sands of the Lake of Gennesaret,[1] where Simon, James, and John were cleaning their nets after a long night of unproductive fishing. For weeks the Galilean countryside had been humming with news of a budding new prophet on Israel's horizon: Jesus of Nazareth.

> And He came down to Capernaum, a city of Galilee. And He was teaching them on the Sabbath; and they were amazed at His teaching, for His message was with authority. (Luke 4:31–32)

This message was not a part of the original series but is compatible with it.

1. "The famous sheet of water in Galilee is called by three names—the Sea of Galilee, the Sea of Tiberias and the Lake of Gennesaret. It is thirteen miles long by eight miles wide. It lies in a dip in the earth's surface and is 680 feet below sea level. . . . Nowadays it is not very populous but in the days of Jesus it had nine townships clustered round its shores, none of fewer than 15,000 people. Gennesaret is really the name of the lovely plain on the west side of the lake, a most fertile piece of land." William Barclay, *The Gospel of Luke*, rev. ed., The Daily Study Bible Series (Philadelphia, Pa.: Westminster Press, 1975), p. 56.

Not only did Jesus' message have authority—it had power as well. The subsequent exorcism of a demon had arrested everyone's attention in a compelling display of that power (vv. 33–35).

> And amazement came upon them all, and they began discussing with one another saying, "What is this message? For with authority and power He commands the unclean spirits, and they come out." And the report about Him was getting out into every locality in the surrounding district. (vv. 36–37)

As a result, the next morning was abuzz with a hive of people gathered around Jesus.

> Now it came about that while the multitude were pressing around Him and listening to the word of God, He was standing by the lake of Gennesaret; and He saw two boats lying at the edge of the lake; but the fishermen had gotten out of them, and were washing their nets. And He got into one of the boats, which was Simon's, and asked him to put out a little way from the land. And He sat down and began teaching the multitudes from the boat. (5:1–3)

Doubtless, the fishermen had heard Jesus speak before, and they, too, had been awed, not only by the persuasiveness of His preaching but also by the power of His presence. Now, as they hunched over their nets, picking them clean of the accumulated debris, Jesus' words penetrated their hearts, making permanent imprints.

The Catch

When Jesus asked Simon to position his boat a little way from shore, Simon and his fishing partners consented. In doing so, they became a captive audience—literally. At the conclusion of His sermon, Jesus planned an object lesson that would be so vivid that the fishermen would never forget its significance.

> And when He had finished speaking, He said to Simon, "Put out into the deep water and let down your nets for a catch." (v. 4)

Simon Peter must have thought Jesus was venturing into waters over His head. After all, fishing was Peter's business, his life; and Jesus was . . . well . . . a preacher.

> And Simon answered and said, "Master, we worked hard all night and caught nothing, but at Your bidding I will let down the nets." (v. 5)

Peter knew the best fishing spots and the most favorable conditions for making a catch, but out of respect for the one he knew as "Master," he did as he was asked. Little did he realize the extent of the Master's domain!

> And when they had done this, they enclosed a great quantity of fish; and their nets began to break; and they signaled to their partners in the other boat, for them to come and help them. And they came, and filled both of the boats, so that they began to sink. (vv. 6–7)

Peter suddenly realized that he stood in the presence of deity. This Jesus was not simply a preacher with the power to heal; He was Lord of the sea and the fish, of every realm, of the entire universe! The words that followed this recognition are reminiscent of the expressions of Abraham, Job, and Isaiah when they, too, stood before the awesome presence of God (see Gen. 18:27; Job 42:5–6; Isa. 6:5).

> But when Simon Peter saw that, he fell down at Jesus' feet, saying, "Depart from me, for I am a sinful man, O Lord!" For amazement had seized him and all his companions because of the catch of fish which they had taken; and so also James and John, sons of Zebedee, who were partners with Simon. (Luke 5:8–10a)

The Objective

As the boats filled with fish, the fishermen's hearts filled with awe. Speechless, they were now primed for what was to prove a life-changing announcement.

> And Jesus said to Simon, "Do not fear, from now on you will be catching men."[2] (v. 10b)

2. The Greek word *zōgreō* means to "catch alive." It appears only one other time in the New Testament, in 2 Timothy 2:26, describing a person "held captive" by the Devil "to do his will." That snaring of humanity will continue until God's people cast their nets and bring those people into the boat of salvation.

Jesus wasn't giving these rough, seasoned fishermen a lesson in fishing; His objective was to change their profession—by changing their lives. And change their lives He did.

> And when they had brought their boats to land, they left everything and followed Him. (v. 11)

Everything? The biggest catch these fishermen had ever made? Their boats? Their nets? Their livelihood? Their homes? Their families? Everything. Without an over-the-shoulder glance. Without even a second thought (compare 9:62).

The Application

The lessons we can apply revolve around three pairs of verbs: *chooses* and *uses*, *moves* and *proves*, *conceals* and *reveals*.

1. *Jesus chooses not to minister to others all alone*. Jesus deliberately involves others in His work. He could have rowed the boat and cast the net Himself, but instead He included the disciples. He didn't want a boatload of spectators; He wanted workers accustomed to rolling up their sleeves, feeling the tug on the nets, and sweating side by side. When He recruited them, He didn't say, "Follow Me, and watch *Me* catch men." He announced, "*You* will be catching men."

How about you? Excellence in the Christian life requires casting our nets into the sea of humanity. Mediocrity lies tanning on the beach, watching the fishing boats of others sail by.

2. *Jesus uses the familiar to do the incredible.* Boats, nets, fish—all quite routine for the fishermen. But it is in the grind of the everyday world where God reveals His glory. What is your world? What is familiar to you? What is your profession or craft? You will be amazed at how the Lord can use you in your sphere of influence to do an incredible work for Him . . . and bring excellence out of even meager and mediocre surroundings.

3. *Jesus moves from the safety of the seen to make us trust Him through the risks of the unseen.* Christ took the fishermen past the shallows and into the deep water to cast their nets. If God is calling you to launch a similar boat of faith and you're teetering on the brink of that decision, don't be afraid to venture out. The Master of the wind and waves is in the boat with you.

4. *Jesus proves the potential by breaking our nets and filling our boats*. The catch of fish in Luke 5 perfectly illustrates God's ability to "do exceeding abundantly beyond all that we ask or think"

(Eph. 3:20). These fishermen had never had such a catch—a catch so great that their nets began to break and their boats began to sink. If you will lay your skepticism aside just long enough to lower your nets, God will amaze you with His ability to fill them.

5. *Jesus conceals His surprises until we follow His leading.* It seemed business as usual for the fishermen to launch their boats and head toward the place where they would cast their nets. The water didn't glow . . . there wasn't a halo around the boat . . . the oars were just as heavy as ever. The surprise didn't come until they put out in deep water and lowered their nets. And that is when Peter realized Jesus was more than just a powerful preacher—He was Lord.

When was the last time God surprised you? When was the last time you took Him at His word and He almost broke your mental nets with a display of His lordship over this world . . . over circumstances . . . over people?

6. *Jesus reveals His objective to those who are willing to relinquish their security.* Only after the disciples gave up the safety of the shore did Jesus finally reveal His purpose: "from now on you will be catching men" (Luke 5:10b). If we are ever to live above the level of mediocrity, we can't be landlubbers hugging the shore. We have to launch out into sometimes deep waters . . . and that means more than dangling our ankles in the shallows. Mediocrity will bid us, like a seductive siren, to rest secure on the shore. But the pursuit of excellence calls us to set sail into the waters of faith.

Living Insights STUDY ONE

It's so easy to leave Jesus safely back in the first century and bring only His principles into our lives today. To counteract this tendency, let's thoughtfully reconstruct Luke's story for the present—your present.

People all around you need to hear Jesus' unique teaching, feel His healing touch, see His power displayed. There's quite a crowd of them, but you may not give them more than a passing glance because you see them all the time. Jesus pays attention to them, though, and He needs a place from which He can be heard. Peter offered Jesus his boat. You probably don't have a boat that Jesus would climb aboard; but you do have a home, a place of work, a familiar arena that could serve as Jesus' platform. Write down what your equivalent of Peter's boat is.

____

Jesus may be looking at you right now and saying, _______ _________ (your name), "put out into deep water . . ." What is your "deep water"?

____

". . . and let down your nets for a catch." What do you think your "nets" might be? Perhaps they are talents or skills; maybe they signify your willingness to take action or extend your trust. See if you can define what yours are and how they relate to your "deep water."

____

____

Are you hesitating to do what the Lord has asked? If so, why?

____

____

What do you need to do? Don't just answer, "Obey." Try to be specific in terms of your situation.

____

____

____

Jesus' purpose in taking Peter and the others out and overflowing their nets and boats was to get their attention, wake them up to the many people ashore whom He wanted to catch for His kingdom. The deep water and the fish were not ends in themselves; they served to illustrate something far greater.

Your "boat" is near a shore of people Jesus wants to "catch." Who are some of them?

_____________________ _____________________

_____________________ _____________________

Jesus is a partner in your business, a member of your family, a friend in your circle—a powerful passenger in your boat. Look at Him, listen to Him, worship Him, follow Him. He knows more than you know, and His goals are greater than you can even dream. Share Him with those people you named above as you would share one who has caught your heart and life with the patient grace of a master fisherman.

Living Insights STUDY TWO

Does this whole idea of deep water and overflowing nets and sharing your faith and leaving everything behind have you a little bit scared? That's understandable. Even the disciples, who saw that miracle and many others with their own two eyes, continued to get scared throughout Jesus' time with them. Remember another time they were together on a boat?

> Now it came about on one of those days, that He and His disciples got into a boat, and He said to them, "Let us go over to the other side of the lake." And they launched out. But as they were sailing along He fell asleep; and a fierce gale of wind descended upon the lake, and they began to be swamped and to be in danger. And they came to Him and woke Him up, saying, "Master, Master, we are perishing!" (Luke 8:22–24a)

"Everything feels out of control—I'm going to die!" Ever feel like that when change and the unknown swirl around you? Most of us have. It's important, then, to pay attention to what Jesus did in response to His disciples' fear.

> And being aroused, He rebuked the wind and the surging waves, and they stopped, and it became calm. And He said to them, "Where is your faith?" And they were fearful and amazed, saying to one another, "Who then is this, that He commands even the winds and the water, and they obey Him?" (vv. 24b–25)

Who then is this? This is your Savior! The all-powerful and ever-living God, who came so you wouldn't perish! He's the filler of your nets, the calmer of your storms.

Maybe one reason we grow fearful is that we are forgetful of who He is and how near He is to us. Take time now to refresh your memory by spending time with Him in prayer. If your faith has been weak, ask Him to forgive that and help you strengthen it. But don't do *all* the talking; in any conversation listening is involved too. So have your Bible open while you pray, and listen for any passages He may lay upon your heart.

Chapter 19

STANDING STRONG WHEN TEMPTED

(PART ONE)

Judges 13:1–12; 14:1–7

Goliath. Nine feet six inches of barbaric might and muscle (see 1 Sam. 17:4). A Philistine fighting machine, he waited in the valley of Elah to challenge the troops of Israel (vv. 8–11).

He stood in defiance, arrayed for battle, wearing a bronze helmet and clothed in scales of overlapping armor weighing more than a hundred pounds (v. 5). Bronze shin guards protected his legs, and a bronze javelin was slung between his shoulders (v. 6). He held a huge spear and had a shield so massive it had to be carried by his armor-bearer (v. 7). Only a small portion of his face was unprotected.

He seemed intimidatingly invincible.

Yet, in a confrontation with a young shepherd boy named David, Goliath would meet not only his match but also his demise. For a well-placed stone from David's slingshot struck the giant at his only point of vulnerability. And he fell, never to rise again.

Like the smooth stones in David's slingshot, the temptations of the world—fame, fortune, power, and pleasure—come at us with powerful force and hit us right between the eyes. These temptations are so direct and lethal that no giant, regardless of how spiritual, is invincible.

As we shall see in this study, one larger-than-life target of temptation was Samson. And the stone that brought about his fall was pleasure—specifically, sexual pleasure.

Samson's Favorable Circumstances

Few babies have come into the world swaddled with such favorable circumstances as Samson. Like John the Baptist and Jesus of Nazareth, his birth was divinely announced.

> And there was a certain man of Zorah, of the family of the Danites, whose name was Manoah; and his wife was barren and had borne no children. Then the angel of the Lord appeared to the woman, and

> said to her, "Behold now, you are barren and have borne no children, but you shall conceive and give birth to a son." (Judg. 13:2–3)

Furthermore, like John and Jesus, Samson was consecrated from birth.

> "For behold, you shall conceive and give birth to a son, and no razor shall come upon his head, for the boy shall be a Nazirite to God from the womb."[1] (v. 5a)

Also like John and Jesus, Samson was given a unique life mission by God.

> "And he shall begin to deliver Israel from the hands of the Philistines." (v. 5b)

To guide him toward that mission, God placed Samson in the home of godly parents specifically chosen for their dedication and stewardship. When Samson's mother received the news that she was to have a child, she rushed to tell her husband, Manoah (vv. 6–7). Manoah wanted to understand his responsibility in rearing this child—he wanted to prepare his son for his divinely appointed mission. So he entreated the Lord to send back the angelic messenger to teach him how to bring up this child, and he listened intently to his instructions (vv. 8, 11–14). Samson's life was off to a great beginning before he ever left the starting block, for he had not only all these benefits but the blessing of God as well.

> Then the woman gave birth to a son and named him Samson; and the child grew up and the Lord blessed him. (v. 24)

Yet that solid start was no guarantee that he would accomplish his mission without breaking his stride. In fact, several hurdles appeared along the way to trip him up.

Samson's Flawed Character

The next time we see Samson, he is fully grown. We are not

1. For the specifics of the Nazirite vow, see Numbers 6:1–8. Essentially, Nazirites had to adhere to a strict diet with no strong drink; they could not cut their hair and could never go near a dead person.

told about the first lap of his childhood, but it is apparent that his passion for God's mission has flagged. As he rounds the turn for the second lap, his spiritual flaws come into plain view—even from the grandstands.

Samson and the Philistine Woman

Samson's lust lures him off the track, enticing him to refresh himself with the forbidden fruit of a Philistine woman.

> Then Samson went down to Timnah and saw a woman in Timnah, one of the daughters of the Philistines. So he came back and told his father and mother, "I saw a woman in Timnah, one of the daughters of the Philistines; now therefore, get her for me as a wife." Then his father and his mother said to him, "Is there no woman among the daughters of your relatives, or among all our people, that you go to take a wife from the uncircumcised Philistines?" But Samson said to his father, "Get her for me, for she looks good to me." (14:1–3)

How telling that the first words we hear from Samson are, "I saw a woman. . . ." Fixing his attention on the wrong objectives was what tripped Samson up. He focuses only on the woman's physical appearance and on pleasing himself. Twice we read in this account that the Philistine woman "looks good" to him (vv. 3, 7). He gives no thought to her character or even her name. Her sexual appeal is all that catches his eye.

It's important to understand that Samson's attraction to the woman's looks was not unique to him. The way men and women are drawn to each other is different, as Dr. James Dobson explains.

> First, men are primarily excited by *visual* stimulation. . . . Women, by contrast, are much less visually oriented than men. . . . Second (and much more important), men are not very discriminating in regard to the person living within an exciting body. A man can walk down a street and be stimulated by a scantily clad female who shimmies past him, even though he knows nothing about her personality or values or mental capabilities. He is attracted by the body itself. . . . Women are much more discriminating

> in their sexual interests. They less commonly become excited by observing a good-looking charmer . . . ; rather, their desire is usually focused on a *particular* individual whom they respect and admire. . . . Obviously, there are exceptions to these characteristic desires, but the fact remains: sex for men is a more physical thing; sex for women is a deeply emotional experience.[2]

Knowing this, men, can help you develop a more precise and powerful strategy against temptation—both in what you are tempted by and in how you may tempt women. And, women, understanding these differences can help you ease a man's battle with the visually enticing—especially in the way you dress—as well as keep you from being tempted by a charmer's smooth touch.

Samson and the Gaza Harlot

Samson was drawn to the Philistine woman by his lust, but God used the match to strengthen his foothold in that nation, helping to fulfill his mission to deliver Israel from the Philistines (v. 4; compare 13:5). For twenty years Samson served as judge over Israel (15:20), apparently ruling with faith and righteousness (see Heb. 11:32–34). Again, however, his focus becomes diverted, and he is drawn off track.

> Now Samson went to Gaza and saw a harlot there, and went in to her. (Judg. 16:1)

C. S. Lewis could have summed up Samson's mistake when he wrote:

> The monstrosity of sexual intercourse outside marriage is that those who indulge in it are trying to isolate one kind of union (the sexual) from all the other kinds of union which were intended to go along with it and make up the total union. The Christian attitude does not mean that there is anything wrong about sexual pleasure, any more than about the pleasure of eating. It means that you must not isolate that pleasure and try to get it by itself,

2. James Dobson, *What Wives Wish Their Husbands Knew about Women* (Wheaton, Ill.: Tyndale House Publishers, 1975), pp. 114–16.

> any more than you ought to try to get the pleasures of taste without swallowing and digesting, by chewing things and spitting them out again.[3]

Samson's preoccupation with physical pleasure is one our society shares—in fact, its gratification has virtually become a national pastime. Lewis marks this as a sign of a culture gone awry.

> There is nothing to be ashamed of in enjoying your food: there would be everything to be ashamed of if half the world made food the main interest of their lives and spent their time looking at pictures of food and dribbling and smacking their lips.[4]

What about you? What's the main interest, the primary preoccupation of your life? Is it the physical—or is it the eternal?

This romp of Samson's with the harlot nearly cost him his life (see 16:1–3; compare Prov. 6:26–28). Yet, as we will see in the next chapter, he jumps right out of the harlot's frying pan into Delilah's fire (Judg. 16:4).

Each snare in this tragic hero's story is tripped by his sensuality, and like the bird that "hastens to the snare" (Prov. 7:23), his following after enticement did finally cost him his life. Samson serves as a graphic symbol of sensuality, and his illicit escapades vividly illustrate James 1:14–15:

> But each one is tempted when he is carried away and enticed by his own lust. Then when lust has conceived, it gives birth to sin; and when sin is accomplished, it brings forth death.

Living Insights — STUDY ONE

Resisting the lure of lust is a tough job; in fact, it's a battle.[5] And that means we need to know our resources, our weapons, and

3. C. S. Lewis, *Mere Christianity*, rev. and enl. (New York, N.Y.: Macmillan Publishing Co., 1952), p. 96.

4. Lewis, *Mere Christianity*, pp. 91–92.

5. This Living Insight, by Bill Butterworth, originally appeared in the study guide *Old Testament Characters*, rev. ed., coauthored by Ken Gire, from the Bible-teaching ministry of Charles R. Swindoll (Fullerton, Calif.: Insight for Living, 1991), p. 17.

our enemy's strategy. In Proverbs, Solomon passed on a battle plan to his sons. Let's familiarize ourselves with his wise directives.

Spend some time reading Proverbs 5–7, keeping your eye out for four specific topics: (1) descriptions of the harlot, (2) descriptions of the fool who succumbs to her, (3) descriptions of the wise man who turns away, and (4) practical advice on how to avoid the harlot.

Descriptions of the harlot: ______________________________

Descriptions of the fool: ______________________________

Descriptions of the wise man: ______________________________

Practical advice: ______________________________

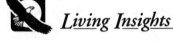

Living Insights STUDY TWO

Temptation is one of the most dangerous battles in the Christian life. Because of this, it will be worth our while to study it on a more personal level.

1. What area of your life poses the greatest threat in regard to temptation?

2. In what setting does this temptation most often occur?

3. Are you accountable to someone? Can you speak freely to a friend about your struggles? How is this helpful?

4. Which of the following Scripture passages can you make your own in your battle to resist temptation? We have provided space for you if you'd find it helpful to write it out.

Proverbs 4:14–18
1 Corinthians 6:18–20
1 Corinthians 10:13
2 Timothy 2:22
Hebrews 2:18
Hebrews 4:15–16

5. Does looking at your circumstances from God's perspective make a difference? In what way?

Talk to God honestly about the temptations you face, and ask for His strength to withstand them.

Chapter 20

Standing Strong When Tempted

(PART TWO)

Judges 14:7–17; 15:20–16:21

Unlatch any fisherman's tackle box and inside you'll find a vast assortment of lures: shiny spinners with treble hooks, hand-tied flies, silver minnows made of balsa to float along the surface, weighted plastic worms with weedless hooks to wend their wiggly way along the bottom.

The goal of all this elaborate subterfuge is to entice some big fish into thinking the bait is dinner. But when the fish takes the bait, it isn't making a move on its next meal; it's making a move onto the next menu—as catch of the day! Whether artificial or real, bait is designed to appeal to the nature of the fish—it is designed to entice.

The word *entice* is found in James 1:14 in an image all fishermen can relate to: "But each one is tempted when he is carried away and enticed by his own lust." The Greek translation means "luring with bait," causing the picture of a fish to spring immediately to mind. As the fish meanders through the labyrinth of sunken tree limbs and mossy fronds, a silver minnow coyly shimmies by. Its scales catch a shaft of sun and send it glinting into the eyes of the waiting fish. That's all the enticement necessary. In a darting second, the fish clamps down on the minnow, only to be reeled into the fisherman's waiting net.

The account of Samson's temptation by Delilah also uses the word *entice* (Judg. 16:5). Like a hungry, unsuspecting fish, Samson is drawn out by the shimmy of Delilah's alluring appeal. Naively the bait is taken; fatefully the hook is set . . . and Samson ends up on a Philistine stringer.

The Unfortunate Example

As we saw in the previous chapter, few have grown up in circumstances as favorable as Samson's. His birth was divinely announced (13:3–5a), his life purpose was clearly spelled out (v. 5b), and his parents were deeply spiritual (vv. 8–12, 15–23). Yet the negatives Samson welcomed into his life offset all the positives he was born with.

Unfavorable Characteristics

Four negatives stand out in Samson's life regarding the man himself, his circumstances, his friends, and his spiritual commitment.

First, *he focused on the wrong objectives*. He concentrated only on a woman's physical appearance and on pleasing himself (14:1–3, 7). He had 20/20 vision when judging a book's cover, but his reading skills were limited when it came to reviewing the book's contents.

Second, *he handled his leisure time carelessly*. Samson's divinely appointed purpose in life was to "begin to deliver Israel" (13:5b). Yet he seemed to have a hard time staying on track. On a detour to visit this Philistine woman that had caught his eye, he took another side road and engaged in the trivial pursuit of propounding riddles while loitering around a Philistine camp (14:5–20). Samson had no business whiling away his time like this when the nation of Israel was desperately awaiting deliverance.

Third, *he developed a close alliance with the wrong crowd*. Samson rubbed social shoulders with the very people he was supposed to subdue. In that crowd, he met Delilah—and made an alliance that would put him frying in a Philistine pan.

> After this it came about that he loved a woman in the valley of Sorek, whose name was Delilah. And the lords of the Philistines came up to her, and said to her, "Entice him, and see where his great strength lies and how we may overpower him that we may bind him to afflict him. Then we will each give you eleven hundred pieces of silver." (16:4–5)

In the words "entice him," we see the chink in Samson's armor, which by now has become a gaping hole, obvious to all—even to his enemies. Delilah's weakness, however, is fortune, and she succumbs readily to its lure.

> So Delilah said to Samson, "Please tell me where your great strength is and how you may be bound to afflict you." (v. 6)

Amused, Samson dances to Delilah's seductive tune, teasing her frivolously at first (vv. 7–12). But the game soon shows signs of getting beyond him when he comes perilously close to revealing the truth (vv. 13–14).

Fourth, *he didn't take his vow seriously*. Frustrated with Samson for toying with her, Delilah nags him relentlessly to find the secret of his strength.

> Then she said to him, "How can you say, 'I love you,' when your heart is not with me? You have deceived me these three times and have not told me where your great strength is." And it came about when she pressed him daily with her words and urged him, that his soul was annoyed to death. So he told her all that was in his heart and said to her, "A razor has never come on my head, for I have been a Nazirite to God from my mother's womb. If I am shaved, then my strength will leave me and I shall become weak and be like any other man." (vv. 15–17)

This negative—Samson's careless treatment of a sacred vow—probably offended God the most. Solomon, in his journal, addresses the seriousness of a vow made to God:

> Do not be hasty in word or impulsive in thought to bring up a matter in the presence of God. For God is in heaven and you are on the earth; therefore let your words be few. . . . When you make a vow to God, do not be late in paying it, for He takes no delight in fools. Pay what you vow! It is better that you should not vow than that you should vow and not pay. (Eccles. 5:2, 4–5)

Samson was taking the Lord for granted—perhaps because he had come to believe that his strength originated within himself rather than with God.

Inevitable Consequences

Sin binds us and blinds us and becomes a demanding taskmaster, forcing our noses to a grindstone of harsh consequences.

> When Delilah saw that he had told her all that was in his heart, she sent and called the lords of the Philistines, saying, "Come up once more, for he has told me all that is in his heart." Then the lords of

> the Philistines . . . brought the money in their hands. And she made him sleep on her knees, and called for a man and had him shave off the seven locks of his hair. Then she began to afflict him, and his strength left him. And she said, "The Philistines are upon you, Samson!" And he awoke from his sleep and said, "I will go out as at other times and shake myself free." But he did not know that the Lord had departed from him. Then the Philistines seized him and gouged out his eyes; and they brought him down to Gaza and bound him with bronze chains, and he was a grinder in the prison. (Judg. 16:18–21)

Two inevitable consequences occur when we bite down on the alluring bait of temptation. First, we are weakened, not strengthened. Second, we become enslaved, not freed.

Just as Gulliver was captured by the Lilliputians, so Samson, while sleeping, became entangled in the Philistines' cords.

The man with great strength suddenly became weak. The man sent to bring victory was now the victim. Such are the inextricably binding effects of sin.

> His own iniquities will capture the wicked,
> And he will be held with the cords of his sin.
> (Prov. 5:22)

Is your sin like a tangle of fishing line . . . knotty, out of hand? If so, be careful—sin has a way of entwining itself around us, and what looks like lightweight line can turn into a boa constrictor, squeezing the life completely out of us.

The Victorious Strategy

To become victor instead of victim, we need to cut through the cords of our sinful habits. The following four-point strategy, the opposite of Samson's actions, can set us free.

We must counteract our natural focus. We should focus on "the hidden person of the heart" (1 Pet. 3:4) rather than on externals (v. 3; compare 1 Sam. 16:7). How's your eyesight? Is it sharpened with eternal perspective? Can you see beyond the externals into the heart of another person?

We must guard our leisure time. Since the Devil never takes weekends off, our spiritual life must stand sentry over our pleasures and passions. Self-control is one of the fruits of the Spirit (see Gal. 5:22–23). Are you controlling your passions, especially during idle moments?

We must screen our close companions. Take a good look at your circle of friends. Are they challenging you or corrupting you? Are they contributing to your spiritual dedication or to your delinquency?

We must uphold our vow to God. Our commitment must be taken seriously. For richer or for poorer, in sickness and in health, for better or for worse, our commitment to God must be steadfast. This is the only way we'll be able to stand strong when tempted—the only way we'll have the strength to pass up the tantalizing bait this world dangles in front of us.

Living Insights STUDY ONE

What tragic irony that a man who let his lustful eyes rule his life would end that life blinded. In his reflection on this chapter in Samson's life, writer Lee Hough draws some meaningful lessons from Samson's experience.

> Samson ended up blind and bound. *Blind*, because he failed to develop his spiritual vision, which would have saved him from the snares of temptation. *Bound*, because he had become enslaved to his own lusts instead of binding his heart to obey God. Take a moment to read Psalm 119:97–105 and Proverbs 2:1–16 to see how spiritual eyesight is developed. What part does prayer play in the process? (See 1 Kings 3:5–14 and James 1:5–8.)[1]

From the Psalms passage, what would you say is involved in developing spiritual eyesight?

1. Lee Hough, from the study guide in Charles R. Swindoll's book *Living Above the Level of Mediocrity* (Dallas, Tex.: Word Publishing, 1989), p. 298.

What crucial element, revealed in Solomon's story in 1 Kings 3:5–14, needs to be added to our knowledge of God's Word?

How does James 1:5 relate to Proverbs 2:3–6? Do wisdom and understanding come as the result of a casual request? What does the Proverbs passage reveal about our values, life goals, and the focus of our energies?

How sharp is your spiritual vision, and to what is your heart bound? If you need to, what changes will you make in order to avoid Samson's fate?

Living Insights STUDY TWO

We'd be doing a pretty mediocre job of discussing mediocrity if we didn't include a time of review! What have been the most significant truths and applications you have learned in this last half of our study? How have they fueled your desire to burn brightly with excellence? By jotting down your thoughts, you will have them readily at hand for those times when mediocrity will try to blow out your flame and leave you stumbling in the dark.

LIVING ABOVE THE LEVEL OF MEDIOCRITY

Combating Mediocrity Requires Fighting Fiercely

Winning the Battle over Greed

Slaying the Dragon of Traditionalism ____________________

____

____

Removing the Blahs from Today ____________________

____

____

Becoming a Model of Unselfishness ____________________

____

____

Resisting Mediocrity Includes Standing Courageously

Standing Alone When Outnumbered ____________________

____

____

Standing Tall When Tested ____________________

____

____

Standing Firm When Discouraged ____________________

____

____

Boats, Nets, Fish, and Faith ____________________

____

____

Standing Strong When Tempted (Part One) ____________________

____

____

Standing Strong When Tempted (Part Two) ___________________

____

____

BOOKS FOR PROBING FURTHER

Ted W. Engstrom, former president of World Vision, retells a poignant story about mediocrity that serves as a modern parable.

> An American Indian tells about a brave who found an eagle's egg and put it into the nest of a prairie chicken. The eaglet hatched with the brood of chicks and grew up with them.
>
> All his life, the changeling eagle, thinking he was a prairie chicken, did what the prairie chickens did. He scratched in the dirt for seeds and insects to eat. He clucked and cackled. And he flew in a brief thrashing of wings and flurry of feathers no more than a few feet off the ground. After all, that's how prairie chickens were supposed to fly.
>
> Years passed. And the changeling eagle grew very old. One day, he saw a magnificent bird far above him in the cloudless sky. Hanging with graceful majesty on the powerful wind currents, it soared with scarcely a beat of its strong golden wings.
>
> "What a beautiful bird!" said the changeling eagle to his neighbor. "What is it?"
>
> "That's an eagle—the chief of the birds," the neighbor clucked. "But don't give it a second thought. You could never be like him."
>
> So the changeling eagle never gave it another thought. And it died thinking it was a prairie chicken.[1]

Can you think of anything more tragic than not fulfilling the destiny God has designed for you? For the eagle, that destiny is soaring across the skies. For you and me, it's living above the level of mediocrity.

1. Ted W. Engstrom, *The Pursuit of Excellence* (Grand Rapids, Mich.: Zondervan Publishing House, 1982), pp. 15–16. Anecdote retold from *What a Day This Can Be*, ed. John Catoir (New York, N.Y.: The Christophers).

God has designed you to fly the skies of excellence—not to scratch and peck and grub around on the ground for insects and seeds. It's high time to get your relationship with the Lord off the ground and up in the air. It's time to look up into the heavens—not at the prairie chickens around you. It's time to spread those wings and fly!

To help create a motivational updraft for those outstretched pinions of yours, here are several books we think you will find helpful. Happy flying!

Engstrom, Ted W. *Motivation to Last a Lifetime*. Grand Rapids, Mich.: Zondervan Publishing House, 1984. It's easy to get winded on our quest for excellence; as a result, many give up the quest altogether. What we lack is motivation. In this small but powerful book, Engstrom offers us not just a second wind but resources to keep us going for a lifetime.

———. *The Pursuit of Excellence*. Grand Rapids, Mich.: Zondervan Publishing House, 1982. In this inspiring book, time management expert Ted Engstrom cuts a wide swath through the tall weeds of mediocrity and charts a fresh path toward excellence. Each chapter includes a workable strategy for producing excellence in every area of our lives.

———. *A Time for Commitment*. Grand Rapids, Mich.: Zondervan Publishing House, 1987. Commitment is a sweaty word—it's a *doing* word, not a *feeling* word. This powerful, convicting book will help you roll up your sleeves for a lifetime of commitment and, in doing so, will change the way you view yourself and the world.

———. *Your Gift of Administration: How to Discover and Use It*. Nashville, Tenn.: Thomas Nelson Publishers, 1983. In this helpful book, the author focuses on excellence for the administrator. If you're a leader who has to juggle projects and people, this book will sharpen the personal and professional skills necessary to keep your projects going and your people growing.

Peterson, Eugene H. *Run with the Horses: The Quest for Life at Its Best*. Downers Grove, Ill.: InterVarsity Press, 1983. The title comes from Jeremiah 12:5—"If you have run with footmen and they have tired you out, Then how can you compete with horses?" In a series of profound reflections on the life of Jeremiah, Peterson explores the quest for life at its best and touches the heart of what it means to be fully and genuinely human.

Sanders, J. Oswald. *Spiritual Leadership*. Revised edition. Chicago, Ill.: Moody Press, 1986. A classic for the past twenty years, this book derives its principles for excellence in leadership directly from the Scriptures rather than borrowing them from the world. True spiritual leadership, the author stresses, is authoritative but not authoritarian.

Schaeffer, Franky. *Addicted to Mediocrity: 20th Century Christians and the Arts*. Westchester, Ill.: Crossway Books, 1981. In this *Campus Life* Book of the Year, Schaeffer provocatively demonstrates how Christians today have sacrificed the artistic prominence they enjoyed for centuries and settled instead for mediocrity. The author offers not only a trenchant critique of Christian commercialism but also some practical direction for recovering the lost gem of artistic excellence.

Stott, John R. W. *The Message of the Sermon on the Mount (Matthew 5–7)*. Downers Grove, Ill.: InterVarsity Press, 1978. This excellent exposition of Matthew 5–7 gives the job description for the follower of Christ who wants to live above the level of mediocrity.

Swindoll, Charles R. *Living Above the Level of Mediocrity: A Commitment to Excellence*. Dallas, Tex.: Word Publishing, 1989. Outlining a strategy of commitment to excellence, this book will motivate you to get your life off the ground and start flying with the eagles.

White, John. *Excellence in Leadership*. Downers Grove, Ill.: InterVarsity Press, 1986. Using Nehemiah as a model, White confronts the crises Christian leaders face today. Watching Nehemiah overcome his obstacles, we can learn how to hurdle our own.

Some of the books listed may be out of print and available only through a library. For those currently available, please contact your local Christian bookstore. Books by Charles R. Swindoll may be obtained through Insight for Living, as well as some books by other authors. Just call the IFL office that serves you.

NOTES

NOTES

NOTES

NOTES

NOTES

Notes

Ordering Information

Living Above the Level of Mediocrity

If you would like to order additional study guides, purchase the cassette series that accompanies this guide, or request our product catalogs, please contact the office that serves you.

United States and International locations:

Insight for Living
Post Office Box 69000
Anaheim, CA 92817-0900

1-800-772-8888, 24 hours a day, 7 days a week
(714) 575-5000, 8:00 A.M. to 4:30 P.M., Pacific time, Monday to Friday

Canada:

Insight for Living Ministries
Post Office Box 2510
Vancouver, BC, Canada V6B 3W7

1-800-663-7639, 24 hours a day, 7 days a week

Australia:

Insight for Living, Inc.
General Post Office Box 2823 EE
Melbourne, VIC 3001, Australia

(03) 9877-4277, 8:30 A.M. to 5:00 P.M., Monday to Friday

World Wide Web:
www.insight.org

Study Guide Subscription Program

Study guide subscriptions are available. Please call or write the office nearest you to find out how you can receive our study guides on a regular basis.

Teach Yourself
VISUALLY

Easy Jewelry Projects

Pocket Edition

by Chris Franchetti Michaels

WILEY

John Wiley & Sons, Inc.

Teach Yourself VISUALLY™ Easy Jewelry Projects, Pocket Edition

Published by John Wiley & Sons, Inc., Hoboken, New Jersey

For general information on our other products and services or to obtain technical support please contact our Customer Care Department within the U.S. at (877) 762-2974, outside the U.S. at (317) 572-3993 or fax (317) 572-4002.

John Wiley & Sons, Inc., also publishes its books in a variety of electronic formats. Some content that appears in print may not be available in electronic books. For more information about Wiley products, please visit us at www.wiley.com.

ISBN: 978-1-118-17137-0

Printed in the United States of America

10 9 8 7 6 5 4 3 2 1

Book production by John Wiley & Sons, Inc., Composition Services

Table of Contents

Rings 73

Introduction

Jewelry making is a very personal and rewarding craft. With some basic supplies and a little creativity, you can adorn yourself, and the people in your life, with beautiful objects that communicate your inner feelings and your sense of style.

When you begin making your own jewelry, you will use many of the same techniques that ancient crafters used thousands of years ago. Your designs will be special because you made them by hand to your own specifications. You will experience the satisfaction of making jewelry you really love (and that fits you exactly the way you want it to), while avoiding the cheaply made, mass-produced jewelry that you see at so many retail stores.

You can save money by making your own jewelry. You will also find that gift-giving becomes far less challenging for the jewelry lovers on your gift lists.

One of the most rewarding aspects of jewelry making is that your creations can match any style you choose. If you love fashion, you can be your own personal fashion jewelry designer. If you're interested in a particular culture, religion, spiritual path, or time in history, your designs can reflect what's important to you. You can even reassemble old jewelry into new, updated designs.

As you work through the projects in this book, allow yourself plenty of time to experiment. Enjoy each new accomplishment, and use your newfound talents to bring more creativity and enrichment into your life.

Bracelets and Anklets

From the simplest of stretch bracelets to a copper cuff, this chapter includes a variety of bracelet projects to suit any wrist, along with a delicate anklet project.

Beaded Stretch Bracelet Set

Beaded stretch bracelets are quick and easy projects once you get the hang of them. They look especially stylish when worn in sets. This project uses a variety of larger vintage Lucite beads for a striking effect and a comfortable fit.

Length: About 7 inches

Tools and Supplies

- Small, sharp scissors or nippers
- Small alligator clamp or Bead Stopper
- E6000 glue
- Paper towels
- Twisted wire needle (optional, if you have trouble stringing the beads without one)

Materials

- $6\frac{1}{2}$ feet of clear .7mm stretch cord
- 16 round Lucite beads in marbled dark avocado (12mm)
- 4 Lucite rings in yellow opal (5mm x 15mm)
- 17 round Lucite beads in light olivine moonglow (11mm)
- 22 round Lucite beads in light olivine moonglow (8mm)
- 2 faceted round cat's-eye glass beads in olive green (10mm)
- 15 round Lucite beads in brown-orange-green stripe (12mm)
- 13 round Lucite beads in lemon-and-white swirl (12mm)
- 4 round Lucite beads in lemon-and-white swirl (8mm)

NOTE: *These materials will make a set of five bracelets.*

Beaded Stretch Bracelet Set
(continued)

Make the Bracelets

1. Following the bead patterns shown, string each bracelet, one at a time, using alligator clamps or Bead Stoppers as necessary to keep the beads from falling off.
2. Tie a square knot in the stretch cord to close each bracelet. Apply a drop of E6000 glue to each knot, and slide each knot into an adjacent bead to conceal it.
3. After the glue has fully set, use sharp scissors to trim off the cord tails.

TIP

Lucite beads are great for stretch bracelets not only because of their interesting style, but also because they are very lightweight. However, you won't be able to find them at every bead store. Most Lucite beads are part of limited supplies of unused vintage materials that specialty suppliers collect. You can find them by searching the Internet and by browsing online auction sites.

Celtic Wirework Charm Bracelet

A basic double jump ring chain makes a perfect base for a charm bracelet. This design has a whimsical, Old-World theme with its Celtic knot and dragon charms. Spiral-end bead-drop charms add color and movement.

Length: 7½ inches

Tools and Supplies

- Side cutters
- Chain nose pliers
- Flat nose pliers
- Round nose pliers
- Knotting board with T-pins (optional)

Celtic Wirework Charm Bracelet *(continued)*

Materials

- 92 silver-tone jump rings, 18 gauge (7mm outside diameter)
- Wirework simple hook clasp made from 18-gauge silver-tone wire
- Wirework simple clasp eye made from 18-gauge silver-tone wire
- 30 inches of 24-gauge silver-tone wire
- 3 pewter dragon charms (23mm)
- 3 Celtic knot disc charms (14mm)
- 5 Celtic knot connectors (14mm)
- 9 Czech fire polish hurricane glass faceted round beads in amethyst-peridot-tortoise (6mm)

NOTE: *For the silver-tone wire, you can use nickel silver, silver-colored copper, or sterling silver.*

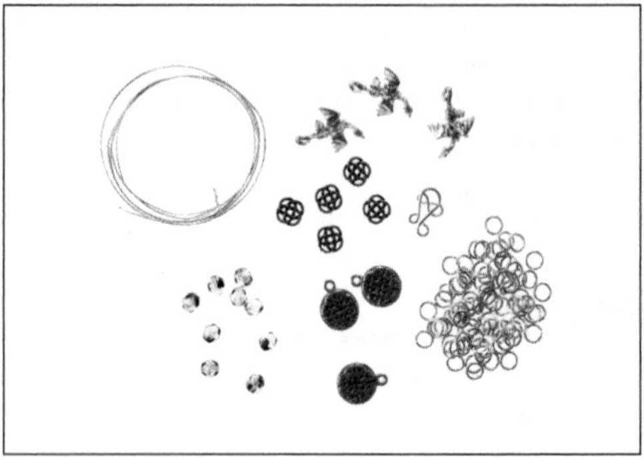

Make the Bracelet

1. Begin with two closed jump rings.
2. Use chain nose pliers to pass an open jump ring through both closed jump rings.

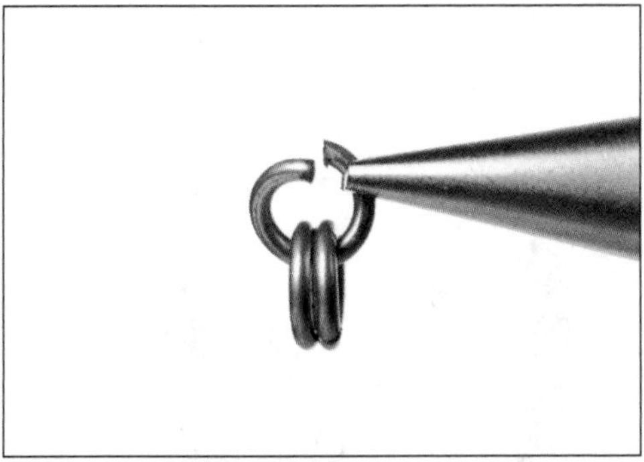

3. Close the open jump ring.
4. Pass another jump ring through the first two closed rings, and close it. You now have two links of chain.

5. Continue adding sets of two jump rings to make a double jump ring chain that contains 37 links.
6. Attach the hook clasp and clasp eye to each end of the chain.
7. Use the 24-gauge wire and Czech glass beads to make nine wrapped bead drops with spiral ends.
8. Lay out the chain neatly on your work surface, with every other link facing the same direction.

NOTE: *If you have trouble keeping the chain from twisting while you work, try anchoring it horizontally to a knotting board with T-pins.*

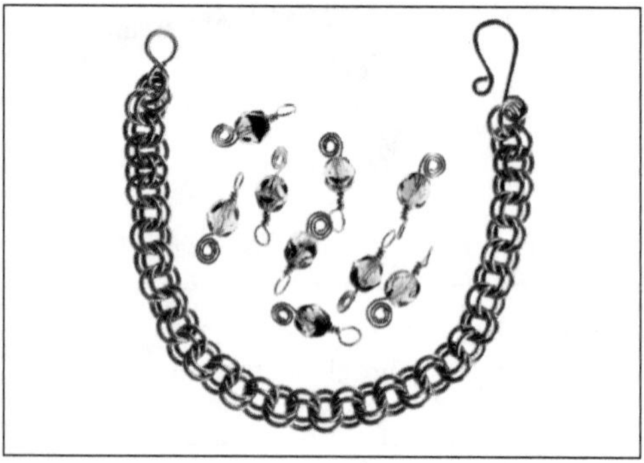

9. Beginning with the second link in the chain, attach a dragon charm to the bottoms of both rings in the link using one of the unused jump rings.
10. Skip the very next link, and attach a bead drop to the bottom of the following link (again using a jump ring).
11. Continue adding charms to the bottom of every other link in the order shown, ending with the third dragon charm.

12 Make a final cluster of three charms by adding the remaining charms to a jump ring and attaching it to the clasp eye.

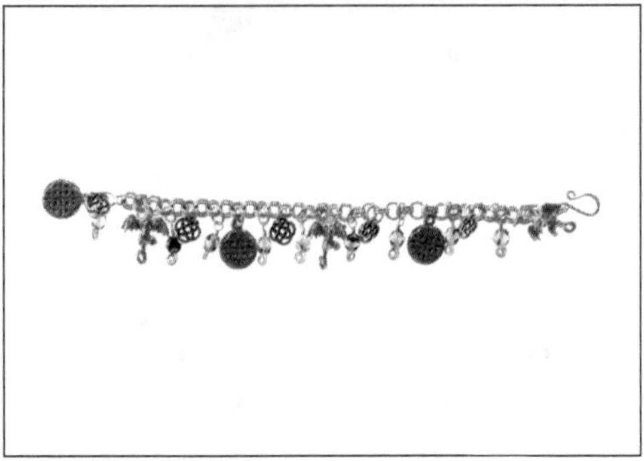

TIP

The double jump ring chain is one of the simplest chains for attaching charms, but you can use more elaborate chains for charm jewelry. S-chains and double-wrapped loop chains both work well. You can even include simple or wrapped bead links within a chain to add color. This technique works especially well for charm necklaces because their longer length allows the charms to be spaced more loosely. If you prefer a fringier look for your charm jewelry, try hanging multiple charms from each link. Just be sure to hold up your work occasionally to make sure that it lies the way you want it to.

Multi-Strand Tin Cup Anklet

This project uses traditional tin cup styling to create a casual anklet that is lightweight, secure, and comfortable to wear. The multiple strands are finished using the traditional beaded tassel-making technique.

Length: About 10½ inches

Tools and Supplies

- Knotting awl, darning needle, or knotting tool
- Handmade folded-card tin cup necklace spacer, ½ inch in length
- Alligator clamp (for securing the spacer)
- Sharp scissors or nippers
- Bead reamer
- E6000 glue

Materials

- 2-meter card of size No. 2 jade green silk cord with attached twisted-wire needle
- 2-meter card of size No. 2 beige silk cord with attached twisted-wire needle
- 2 carved latticework wood beads (10mm)
- 25 chartreuse green off-round pearl beads (5mm)
- 9 light-bronze round seed pearl beads (4mm)
- 2 brass or gold-tone jump rings, 18 gauge (4mm outside diameter)
- Wirework toggle clasp (T-bar and eye) made with brass or gold-tone wire

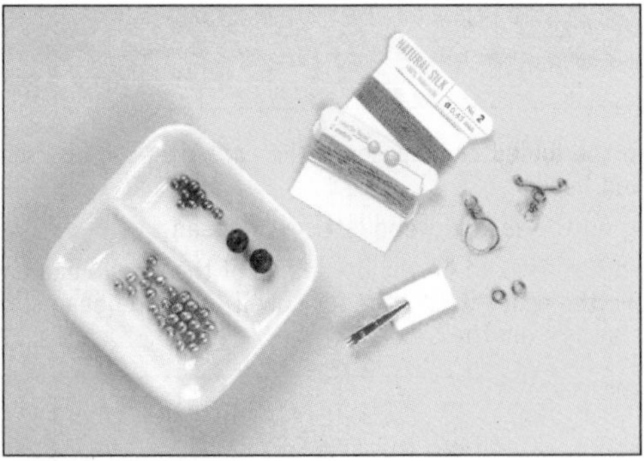

Make the Anklet

1. Remove all the jade green silk cord from its card and give it a couple of gentle tugs to help straighten it out.
2. Tape off the cord about 6 inches from the end and string on one of the wood latticework beads.
3. Use the folded-card spacer and the knotting tool to make a knot in the cord ½ inch away from the wood latticework bead.

Multi-Strand Tin Cup Anklet
(continued)

4. String on the first chartreuse pearl bead.
5. Make another knot to hold the bead in place.
6. Continue using the folded-card spacer to space and knot nine more chartreuse pearl beads.

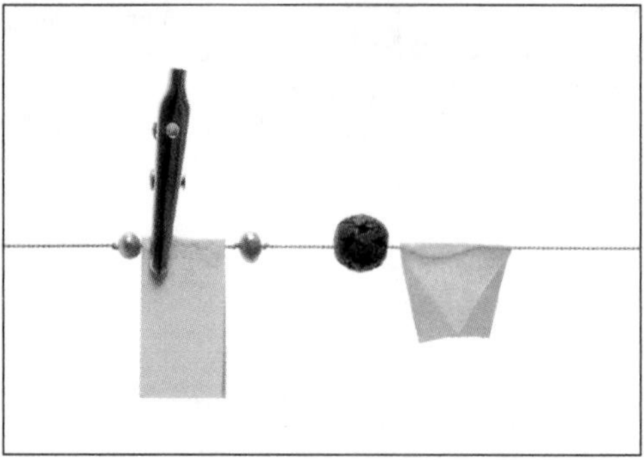

7. Clamp the folded-card spacer to the cord after the last set of knotted beads.
8. String on the second wood latticework bead.
9. Tape off the strand on the other side of the wood bead and remove the spacer. (It's fine for now if the wood bead slides down away from the tape.)

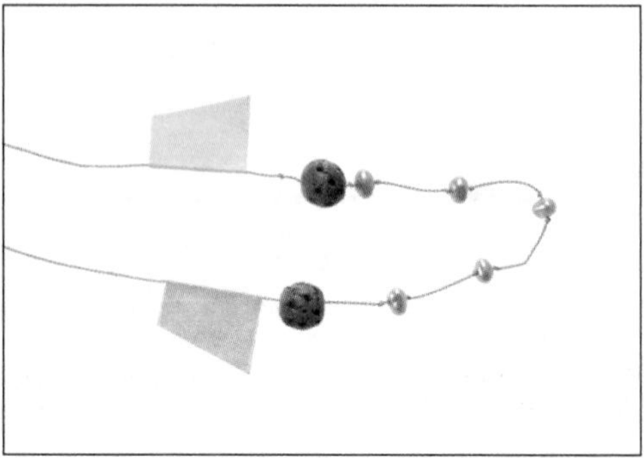

10. Trim the cord about 6 inches away from the tape that you applied in Step 9.
11. Remove all the beige cord from its card and tug it a little to help straighten it. Tape it off about 6 inches from the end as you did with the green cord.
12. Thread the cord through the wood latticework bead that you strung onto the first strand in Step 2. Now both strands are strung through the first wood bead together, and both are taped off behind the wood bead.
13. Use the folded-card spacer and the knotting tool to make a knot ½ inch away from the wood latticework bead. Continue adding beads and knots to complete the strand.
14. When you finish all of the knotted beads for the second strand, clamp on the folded-card spacer again.
15. Thread the cord through the wood bead on this end (the one that you strung onto the first strand in Step 9).
16. Tape off the second strand on the other side of the wood bead, as you did with the first strand.
17. Use the same method to add the third strand of cord following the pattern in the example. Now all three strands are knotted and beaded, and their ends are strung through each of the two wood latticework beads.

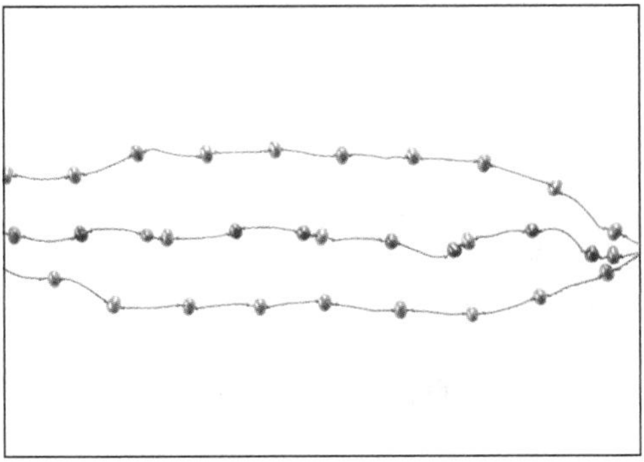

18 Beginning at one end, remove the tape from all three strands.

19 Thread a jump ring over all three cord ends. Make a double overhand knot to secure the jump ring in place.

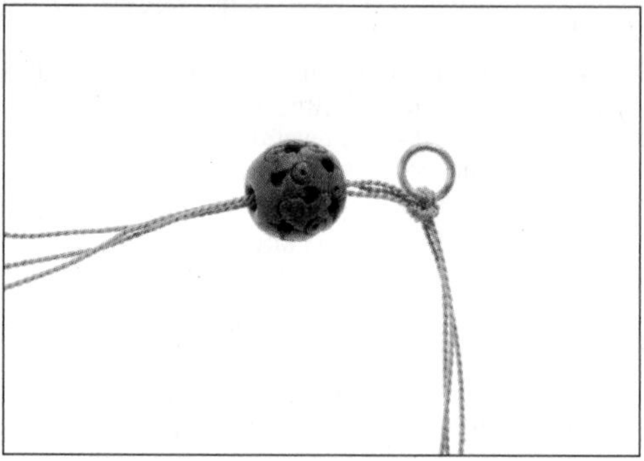

20 Place a tiny drop of E6000 glue on the knot and slide the wood bead over it.

21 Repeat steps 19–20 on the other side of the anklet.

22 Allow the glue at both ends to set.

23 Trim off the extra cord tails at the inside edge of each wood bead.

24 Attach the clasp parts to the jump rings.

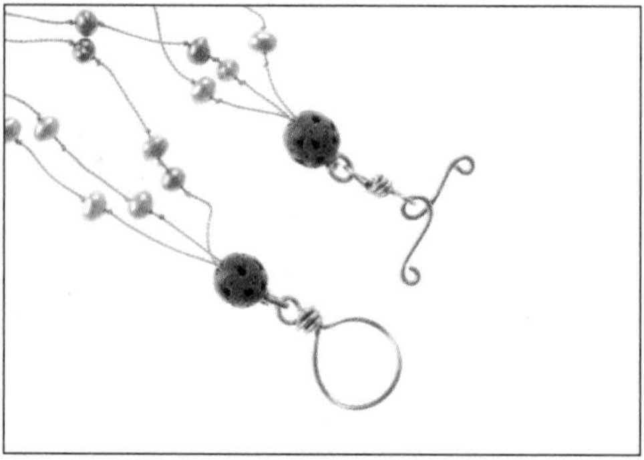

Wirework Bead Cuff Bracelet

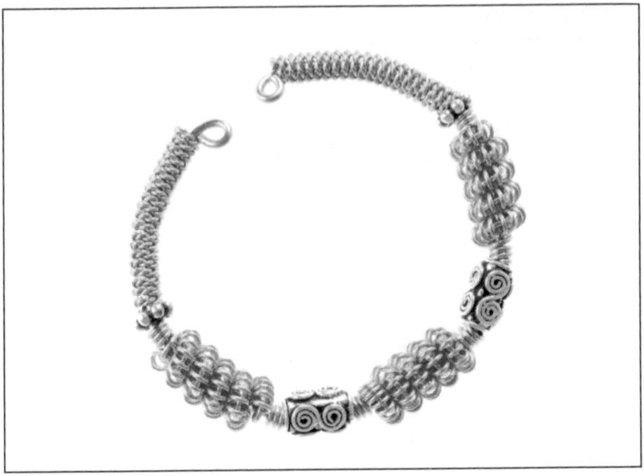

This cuff bracelet design features double-twisted wire, double-wrapped wire beads, and ornate, handmade sterling-silver beads from Bali. You can make it using copper wire as shown, or sterling-silver wire for a more formal look.

Length: Adjustable

Tools

NOTE: *Because 14-gauge wire is thick and takes extra force to bend and cut, always use strong, good-quality tools when you work with it.*

- Round nose pliers
- Heavy-duty side cutters
- 2mm round mandrel
- Bracelet mandrel (or bracelet mandrel substitute)
- Needle file

Wirework Bead Cuff Bracelet *(continued)*

Materials

- 8¼-inch length of 14-gauge copper wire
- Three 29-inch lengths of 20-gauge copper wire
- Three 7-inch lengths of 18-gauge copper wire
- Two 12-inch lengths of double-twisted copper 20-gauge wire with 15 twists per inch
- 2 sterling-silver scroll-design Bali beads (12mm x 7mm)
- 2 sterling-silver daisy-spacer Bali beads (2.5mm x 8mm)

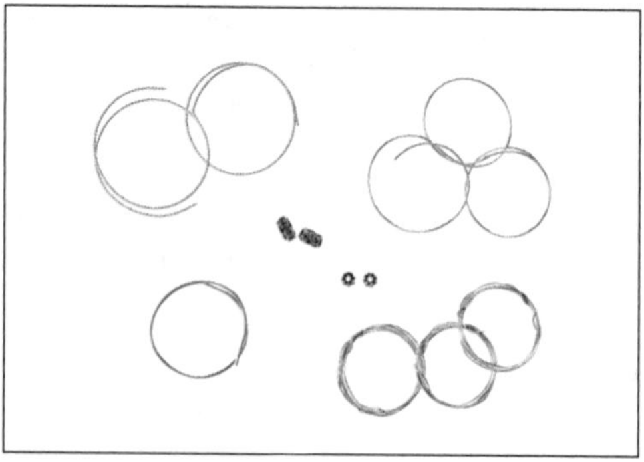

Make the Bracelet

1. Create three double-wrapped wire beads using the three 29-inch lengths of 20-gauge wire, the three 7-inch lengths of 18-gauge wire, and the 2mm mandrel.
2. Wrap each 12-inch length of double-twisted wire snugly around the mandrel to create two 1¼-inch coils.

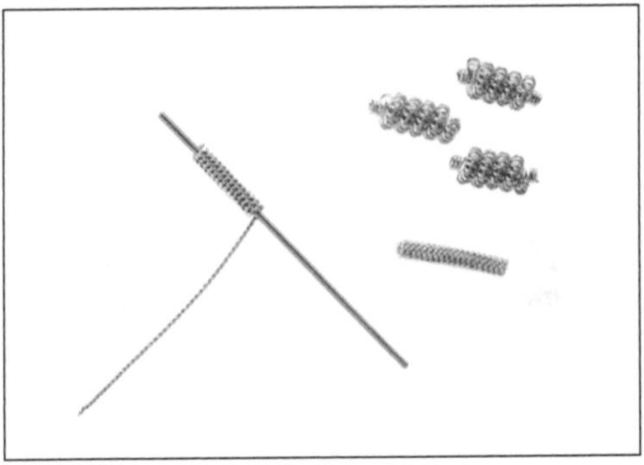

3. Use round nose pliers to create a loop at one end of the 14-gauge wire.
4. String each component onto the 14-gauge wire in the order shown.
5. Use the round nose pliers to create a loop at the other end of the 14-gauge wire.

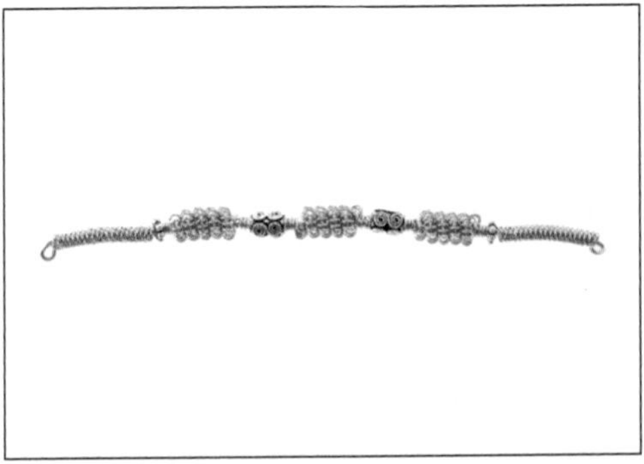

6. Use a bracelet mandrel (or bracelet mandrel substitute) to bend the bracelet into a round shape.
7. Perfect the cuff-bracelet shape by bending the bracelet gently inward with your fingers.

Beaded Framework Link Bracelet

This bracelet is made up of beaded framework links that are formed using a jig and round nose pliers. Copper is a good choice for this design because it is soft enough to bend at a larger gauge, and it is much more economical than sterling silver.

Length: About 7½ inches

Tools

- Wire jig made of metal
- Round nose pliers
- Heavy-duty side cutters
- Needle file
- Chain nose pliers
- Flat nose pliers
- Nylon jaw pliers

Materials

- Six 10-inch lengths of 24-gauge copper wire
- Six 12-inch lengths of 24-gauge copper wire
- Six 5½-inch lengths of 14-gauge copper wire
- About 375 mixed-color Czech glass seed beads in a variety of sizes
- 2 jump rings, 14 gauge (10mm outside diameter)
- 2 wirework hook clasps made with 16-gauge copper wire, with loops large enough to fit loosely over 14-gauge jump rings

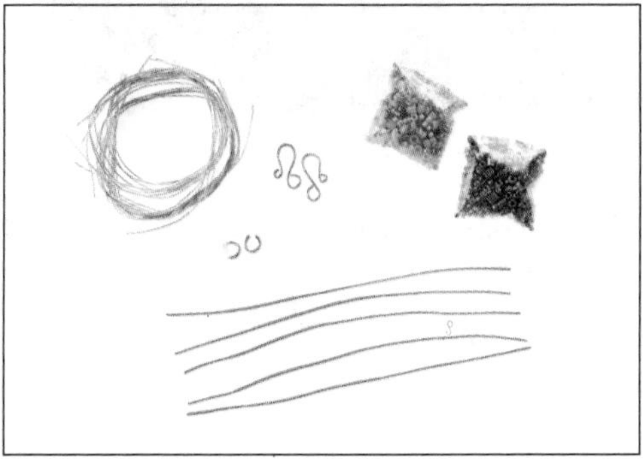

Make the Links

1. Arrange four medium-sized pegs on the jig in a square formation about ⅜ inch apart.
2. Center one 5½-inch length of 14-gauge wire along one side of the square formation.

Beaded Framework Link Bracelet *(continued)*

3. Bend the 14-gauge wire around all four pegs, as shown. One side of the square will have double wire.

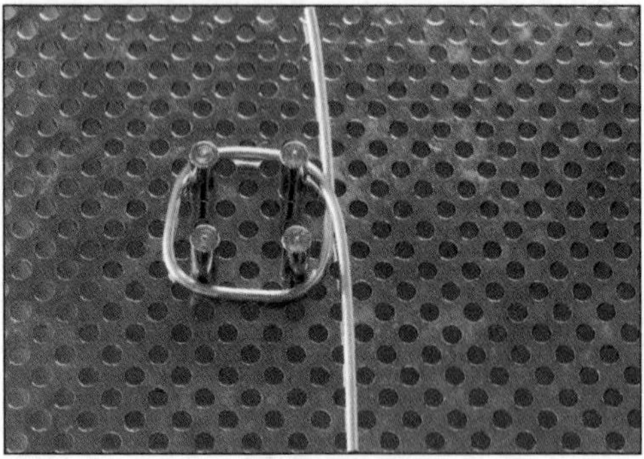

4. Remove the wire from the jig.
5. If necessary, use flat nose pliers or nylon jaw pliers to straighten the sides of the square you just made.
6. Holding the double wire together with your fingers, use a 10-inch length of 24-gauge wire to wrap both wires together at the center, creating about a ½-inch length of wraps.

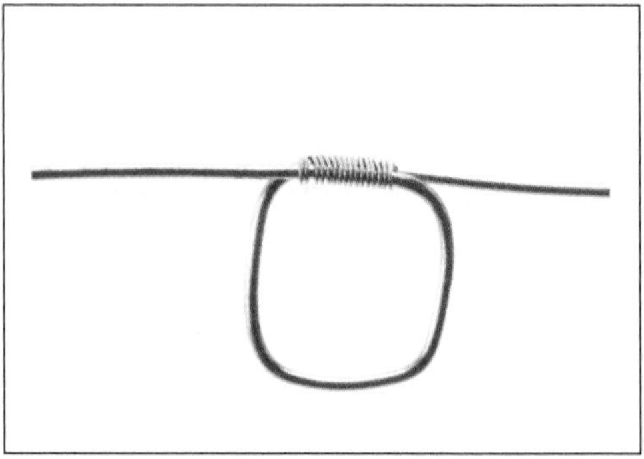

7 Trim off any extra 24-gauge wire at each end of the wraps, and use chain nose pliers to flatten the ends against the 14-gauge wire.

8 Grasp one end of the wrapped wires with flat nose pliers and bend the 14-gauge wire tail to a 90-degree angle.

9 Repeat Step 8 on the other end of the wraps.

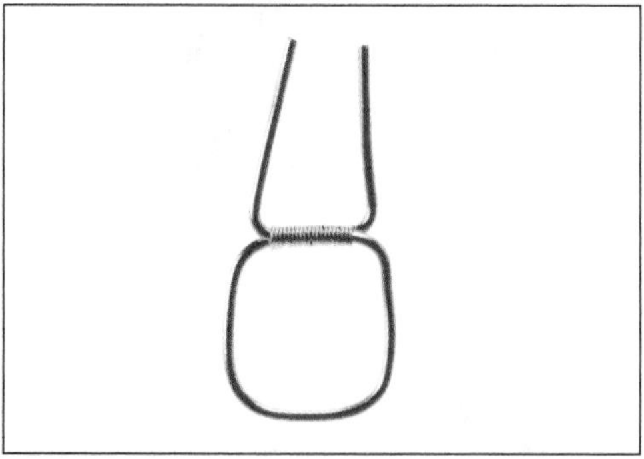

10 Use a needle file to smooth the edges of the wire tails, as needed.

11 Using a length of 12-inch 24-gauge wire, wrap the link with coordinating mixed Czech glass beads, leaving a space of about ⅛ inch at each end of the link. Use the nylon jaw pliers as needed to straighten the wire as you work.

12 Repeat these steps to complete a total of six framework links.

Connect the Links

1 Using round nose pliers, convert both 14-gauge wire tails on each framework link into loops that point in the same direction.

2 Use flat nose pliers to gently open each loop.

Beaded Framework Link Bracelet *(continued)*

3. Connect the links by inserting non-looped ends into looped ends, and using flat nose pliers to close each loop as you go.

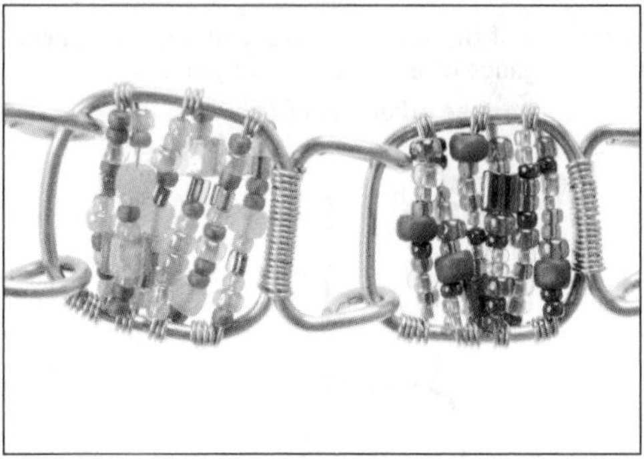

Attach the Clasp

1. Attach the two 14-gauge jump rings to the non-looped end of the last framework link.
2. Attach the two 18-gauge wire-hook clasps to the loops on the first framework link. You can now fasten the bracelet by inserting the hook clasps into the jump rings on the other end.

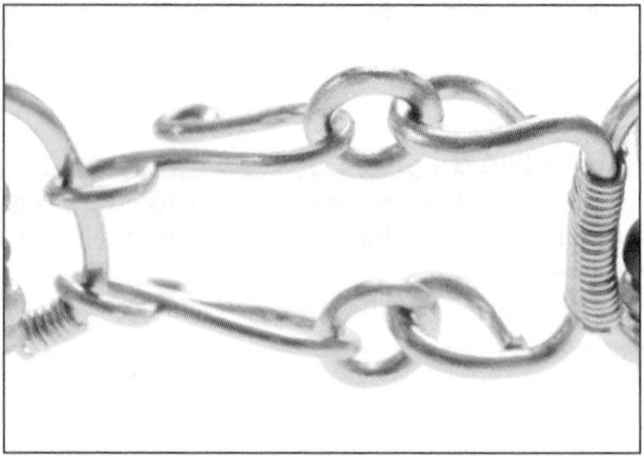

Necklaces

Whether you're interested in making something lovely and feminine or you would like to make a rugged piece for a man to wear, you'll find a variety of appealing necklace designs in this chapter.

Hill Tribe Silver and Gemstone Necklace

The Hill Tribe people of northern Thailand are renowned silversmiths. Their silver beads and jewelry are popular for their artistry and unique, rough-hewn style. This amazonite gemstone necklace features ornate Hill Tribe silver beads and a coordinating floral pendant.

Length: Approximately 16 inches, including the clasp

Tools

- Small side cutters or nippers
- Chain nose pliers
- Flat nose pliers
- Small alligator clamp or Bead Stopper

Materials

- 18 inches of 19-strand, .015-inch-diameter beading wire
- 2 sterling-silver crimp tubes (2mm)
- 2 sterling-silver Wire Guardians
- 76 faceted briolette amazonite beads (6mm x 10mm)
- 44 Hill Tribe silver hollow-saucer spacer beads (2mm x 3.5mm)
- 2 Hill Tribe silver vertical floral beads (10mm x 12mm)
- Hill Tribe silver flower pendant
- Hill Tribe silver toggle clasp
- 2 sterling-silver jump rings, 18 gauge (6mm outside diameter)

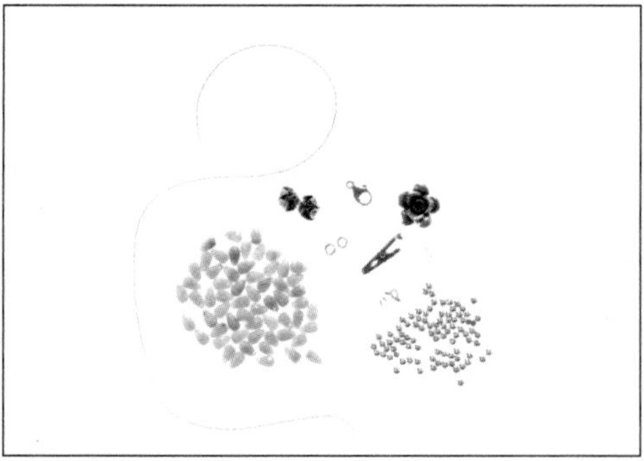

Make the Necklace

1. Affix an alligator clamp or Bead Stopper near the middle of the strand of beading wire.
2. On one end of the strand, string on one hollow-saucer spacer bead, one crimp tube, and a second hollow-saucer spacer bead, in that order.
3. String on a Wire Guardian.

4. Thread the beading wire back down through the beads and crimp tube.
5. With the beads still positioned beneath the Wire Guardian, use chain nose pliers to flatten the crimp tube.

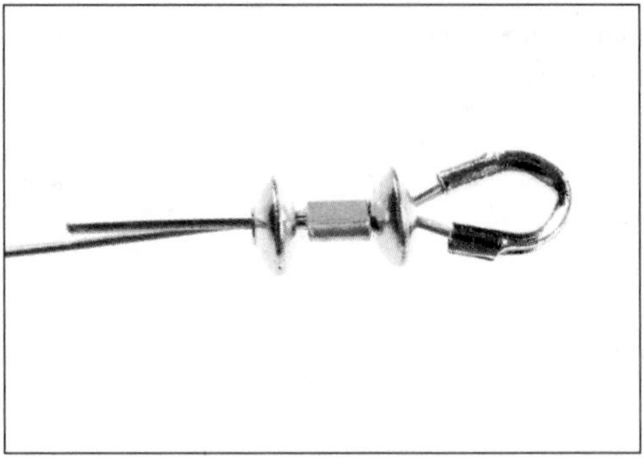

6. Trim the beading wire tail at the base of the bottom spacer bead using small wire cutters or nippers.
7. Remove the alligator clamp or Bead Stopper from the beading wire.
8. String on two amazonite briolette beads and one spacer bead.
9. Continue adding two briolettes and one spacer bead until you have strung a total of 26 briolettes, ending with a final spacer bead.

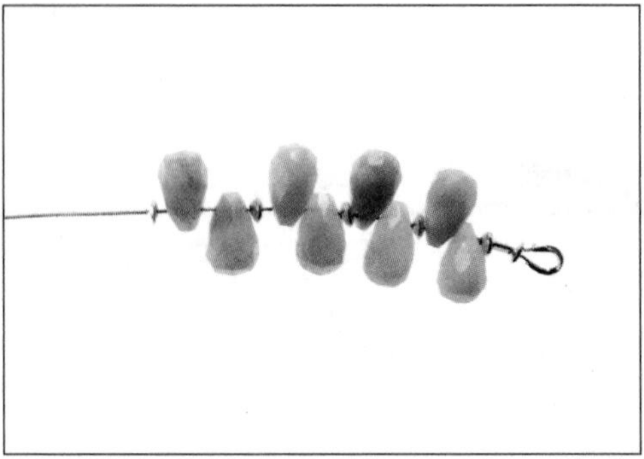

10. String on one 10mm x 12mm Hill Tribe silver floral bead and one more spacer bead.
11. String on 12 more briolettes, with a spacer bead between each set of two briolettes, again ending with a final spacer bead.
12. String on the Hill Tribe flower pendant.
13. String on another spacer bead, and then string on the rest of the beads and the second Wire Guardian to match the first side of the necklace.
14. Thread the beading wire back down through the beads and crimp as you did in Step 4.
15. Flatten the crimp tube with chain nose pliers.
16. Trim the wire tail as you did in Step 6.
17. To finish the necklace, use chain nose pliers in conjunction with flat nose pliers to attach a toggle clasp part to each end with jump rings.

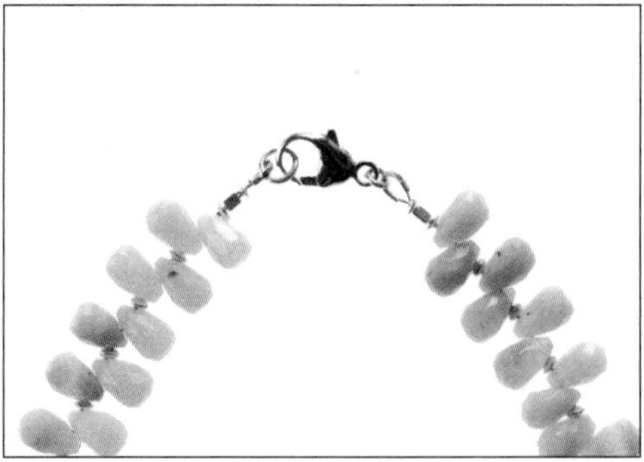

Men's Rugged Leather and Bead Necklace

Men's jewelry typically has a rugged, masculine look. You can achieve this style easily by using leather cord and tribal-style, handmade beads. The beads in this project were made in Africa. Notice how the variety of materials in this design adds interesting texture to its basic color palette.

Length: Approximately 18 inches

Tools

- Scissors or nippers

Materials

- 33 inches of brown Greek leather cord (1.8mm)
- 22 coco shell beads (2mm x 10mm)
- 10 dyed and painted bone beads (24mm x 9mm)
- 20 African handmade copper spacer beads (4mm x 6mm)
- 27 ostrich shell heishi beads (2mm x 10mm)
- 9 brick-red African glass heishi beads (2mm x 9mm)

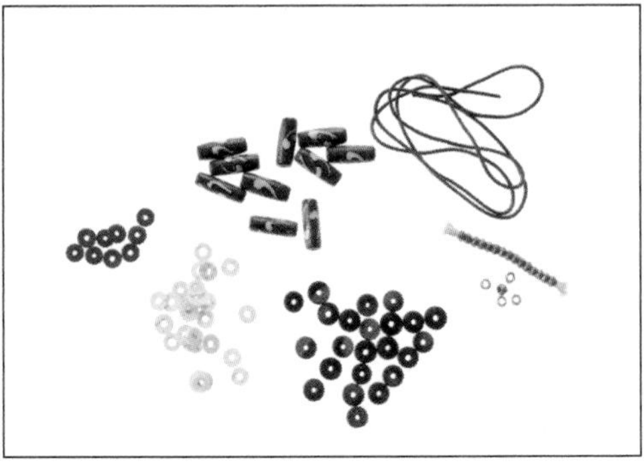

Make the Necklace

1. Tie a secure overhand knot about 1 inch from one end of the leather cord.
2. String on two coco shell beads.
3. Tie a second overhand knot against the coco shell beads.
4. String on the rest of the beads in the pattern shown.

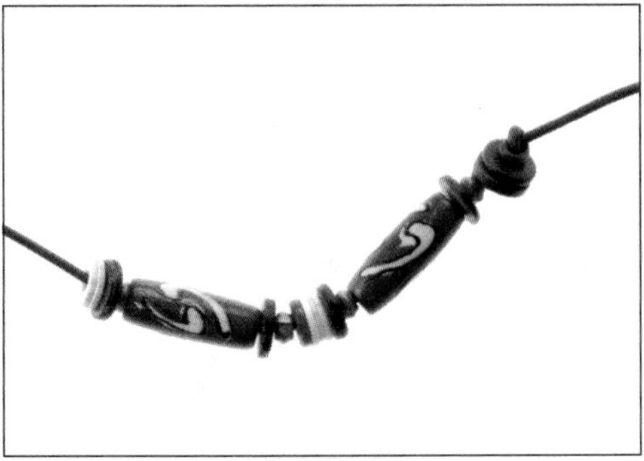

Men's Rugged Leather and Bead Necklace *(continued)*

5. Tie an overhand knot after the final bead.
6. Fold over the remaining tail of cord to form a loop.
7. Tie a loose overhand knot in the doubled cord.
8. Position the knot close to the overhand knot that you made in Step 5, while adjusting it to create a loop slightly larger than the width of the two coco shell beads that you strung on in Step 2.
9. When the loop is the proper size, pull it tight.
10. Trim off the excess cord tail at each end of the necklace, leaving tails about 1 inch long.

TIP

Although this necklace design uses its own built-in clasp, you can also use pre-made findings to finish bead and cord necklaces. End pieces like coil ends and end caps are great alternatives, and they allow you to use jump rings to attach the clasp pieces of your choice.

Beaded Multi-Knot Hemp Choker

This design uses high-quality bleached hemp cord to create small, tight knots with a more even look than natural twine. The pale cream color of the cord nicely accents the blue and green ceramic beads, and the lightweight fish-vertebrae beads add texture.

Length: Approximately 14½ inches

Tools and Supplies

- Sharp scissors or nippers
- Yardstick and/or ruler
- Knotting board with T-pins
- Masking tape

Materials

- 6 yards of .9mm, 10-pound test bleached hemp twine cord
- 6 fish-vertebrae beads (4mm x 8mm)
- 4 kaolin ceramic beads in chartreuse (6mm x 7mm)
- Two 4-sided glazed ceramic tube beads in blue and brown
- Carved black jade convex-tube focal bead (15mm x 12mm)
- 2 copper jump rings, 18 gauge (6mm outside diameter)
- Wire fold-over clasp made with 20-gauge copper wire
- Wire-wrapped clasp eye made with 20-gauge copper wire

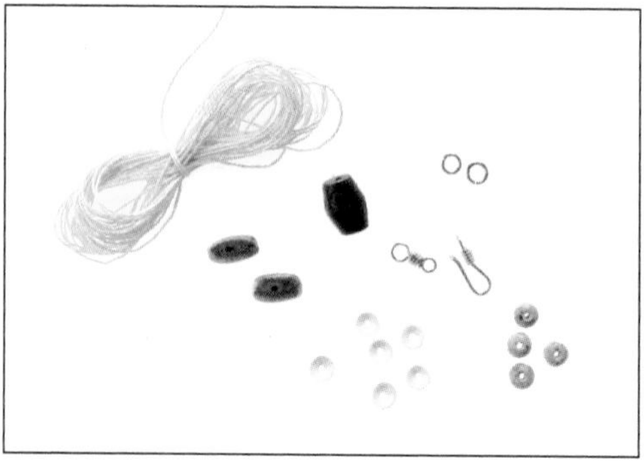

Make the Choker

1. Cut the hemp cord into the following lengths:
   - One 4-yard length (for the working cords)
   - One 1½-yard length (for the filler cords)
   - Two 9-inch lengths (for the wrapping cords)

2. Fold the 4-yard and the 1½-yard lengths in half and hold them together.
3. Use a lark's head knot to attach the cords to one jump ring.

NOTE: *You can find instructions for the knots used in this project after the instructions for making the necklace.*

4. Anchor the jump ring to the knotting board with a T-pin.

5. Make a ¼-inch-long wrap knot around all four cords just below the jump ring, and trim off the cord tails.
6. Make about 1 inch of macramé square knots.
7. String a fish-vertebrae bead vertically onto the filler cords.
8. Make about ⅞ inch of half knots.
9. String another fish-vertebrae bead vertically onto the filler cords.
10. Make about ⅞ inch of macramé square knots.
11. String a kaolin ceramic bead horizontally onto the filler cords.
12. Make another ⅞ inch of half knots.

13. String a four-sided ceramic bead vertically onto the filler cords.

14. Make about 3/8 inch of macramé square knots.
15. String on another vertical fish-vertebrae bead.
16. Make another 3/8 inch of macramé square knots.
17. String on another horizontal kaolin ceramic bead.
18. Make two square knot picots.
19. String the jade focal bead vertically onto the filler cords.
20. Complete the second half of the choker by knotting and stringing beads in reverse order of the first side.
21. String on the second jump ring.
22. Fold over all four cords about 1/2 inch from the last macramé square knot.
23. Using the wrap cord, make a 1/4-inch-long wrap knot around all four cords between the last macramé square knot and the jump ring, and trim off the excess cord tails.

24 Open each jump ring and attach the clasp and clasp eye.

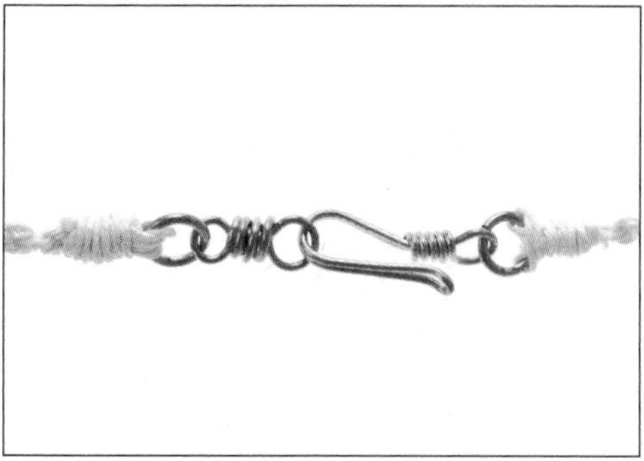

TIP

To make this choker longer, increase the number of square knots you make in steps 6 and 14.

Lark's Head Knot

A lark's head knot folds over an anchor cord to create two strands of working cord.

1 Double over the working cord and place the folded end on top of the anchor cord.

2. Tuck the folded end of the working cord downward beneath the anchor cord to create a downward loop.

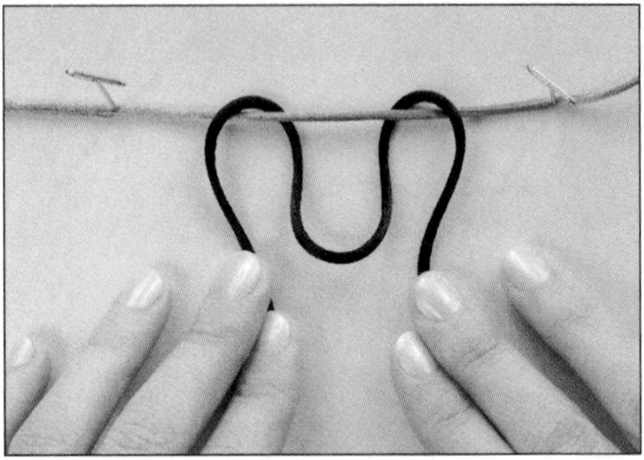

3. Insert both strands of the working cord into and through the folded portion.

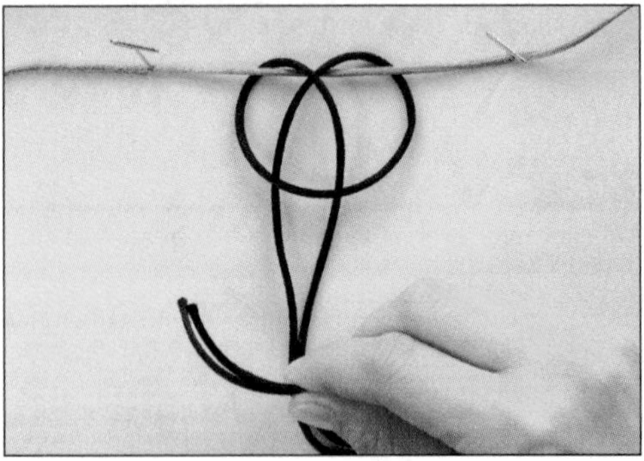

4. Holding the top of the working cord with your fingers, gently pull down on its two strands to tighten the knot.

Wrap Knot

To make a wrap knot, you wrap one cord around a group of other cords to hold them neatly together.

1. Anchor the top ends of the working cords (the black cords shown below) to your work surface. These are the filler cords for the wrap knot.
2. Fold over about 2 inches of the wrapping cord on one end to create a long loop. Position the loop parallel to and against the filler cords.
3. Hold the base of the wrapping cord loop closed and against the filler cords with the fingers of one hand.

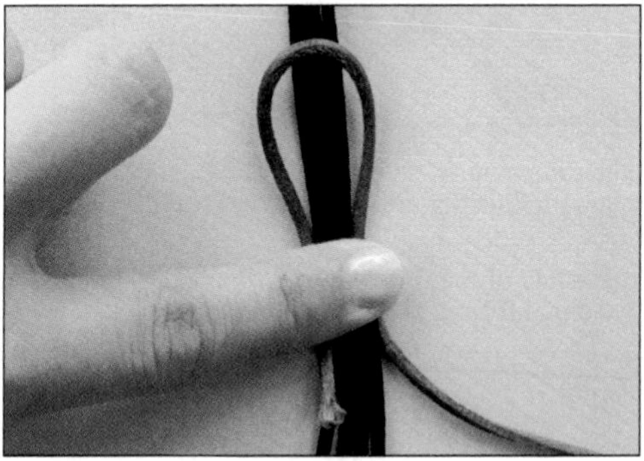

4. With the other hand, wrap the other end of the wrapping cord around all of the filler cords at the base of the loop, leaving about ½ inch of unwrapped tail at the bottom of the loop.

5. Continue wrapping around the filler cords, and the loop itself, in an upward direction until the wraps almost reach the top of the loop.
6. Insert the end of the wrapping cord into and through the loop, and pull it taut.

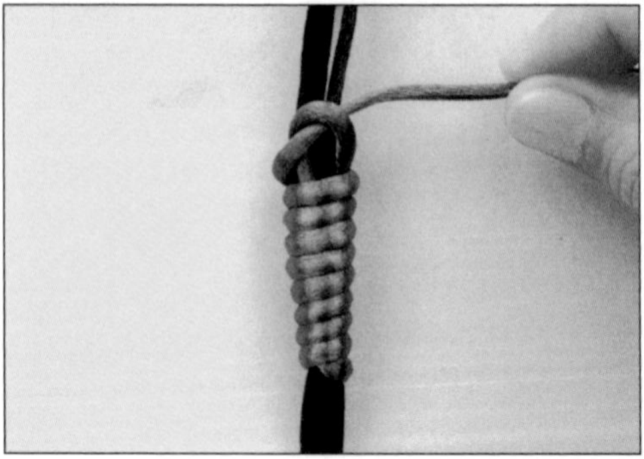

7 Release the top end of the wrapping cord from your fingers and pull on the bottom tail until the top of the loop is positioned completely inside the wraps. Trim off the extra cord tails at both ends.

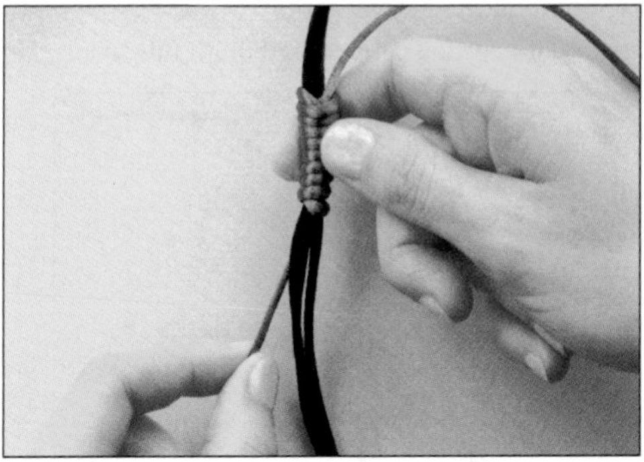

Half Knot

A half knot uses two filler cords and two knotting cords.

1 Attach two working cords to an anchor cord using lark's head knots (see above).

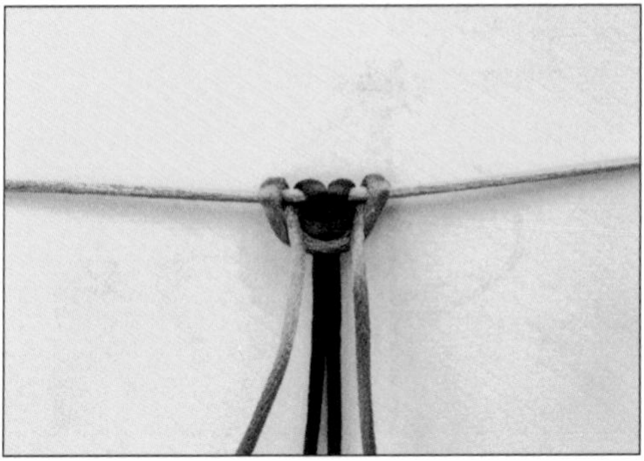

2 Slide the lark's head knots together on the anchor cord so that they are side by side. You now have four strands of working cord.

3 Anchor the two middle strands to your work surface. These are the left and right filler cords; the loose cords are the left and right knotting cords.

4 Tuck the right knotting cord beneath both filler cords.

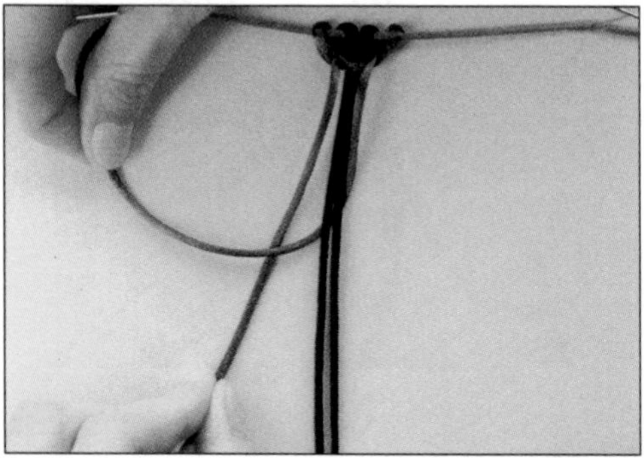

5 Position the right knotting cord over the left knotting cord.

6 Bring the left knotting cord over both filler cords, and tuck it beneath the right knotting cord.

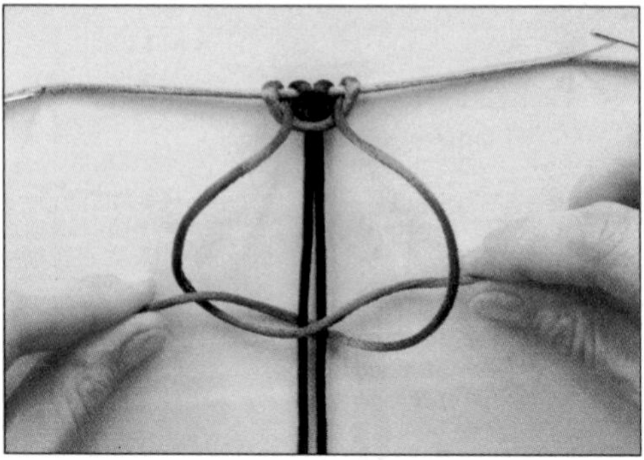

7 Simultaneously pull both knotting cords to their respective sides to tighten the half knot.

Macramé Square Knot

A macramé square knot consists of two half knots tied in opposite directions.

1. Beginning with two filler cords and two knotting cords, tie a half knot (see above).
2. Bring the left knotting cord over both filler cords.
3. Position the left knotting cord over the right knotting cord.
4. Pull the right knotting cord over both filler cords, and tuck it beneath the left knotting cord.

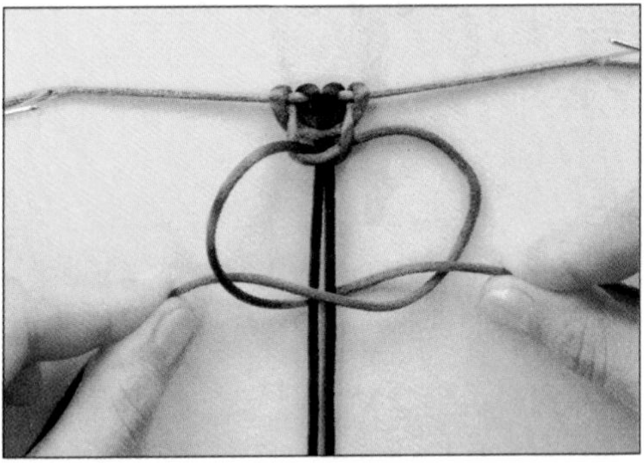

5. Simultaneously pull both knotting cords to their respective sides to tighten the second half of the macramé square knot.

Square Knot Picot

A picot is a length of cord that has been left loose between two knots.

1. Tie a square knot (see above).
2. Insert two T-pins into your work surface at an equal short distance from the filler cords on either side of the cords.
3. Position both knotting cords around the T-pins.

4. Tie another square knot below the T-pins.

5. Remove both T-pins and position the second square knot up against the first one.

Briolette Pendant Ribbon Necklace

Organza ribbon makes an elegant base for wire pendants that are made with a jig. This design features a spiraled variation of the Celtic knot connector, accented with pretty, wrapped gemstone briolettes.

Length: Your choice

Tools and Supplies

- Wire jig
- Sharp scissors
- Side cutters
- Round nose pliers
- Flat nose pliers
- Chain nose pliers
- Masking tape

Materials

- Enough ½-inch-wide, olive organza ribbon to create a three-strand necklace in the length of your choice
- 3 faceted natural agate briolettes, 1 pale and 2 dark (8mm x 12mm)
- Faceted carnelian briolette (8mm x 12mm)
- 11 inches of 26-gauge gold-colored copper wire
- 4½ inches of gold-colored copper wire, 20 gauge
- 8¼ inches of gold-colored copper wire, 18 gauge, blunt-cut at both ends
- 4 gold-colored jump rings, 18 gauge (4mm outside diameter)
- 2 gold-colored jump rings, 18 gauge (4.5mm outside diameter)
- 2 gold-tone end cones (19mm x 6mm)
- Wirework S-hook made from 18-gauge gold-colored copper wire
- Wirework clasp eye made from 20-gauge gold-colored copper wire

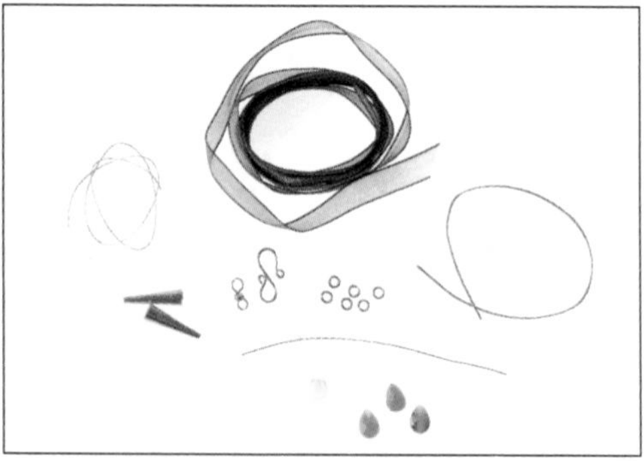

Make the Bail

1. Using 18-gauge wire directly from the coil or spool, wrap the end of the wire around a large peg in the jig to create a large loop.
2. Use side cutters to trim off the excess wire and make the end of the wire blunt.
3. Use your fingers to close the loop.
4. Trim the loop off of the coil or spool, making a blunt cut about 14mm below the loop.
5. Using round nose pliers, make a small loop below the large loop, facing the opposite direction.

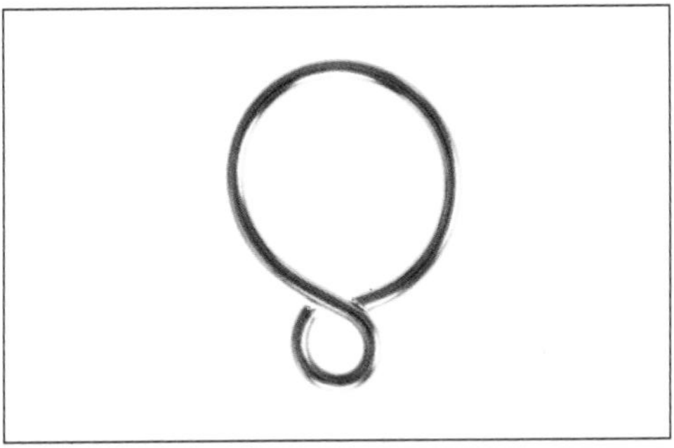

Celtic Knot Wire-Jig Pattern

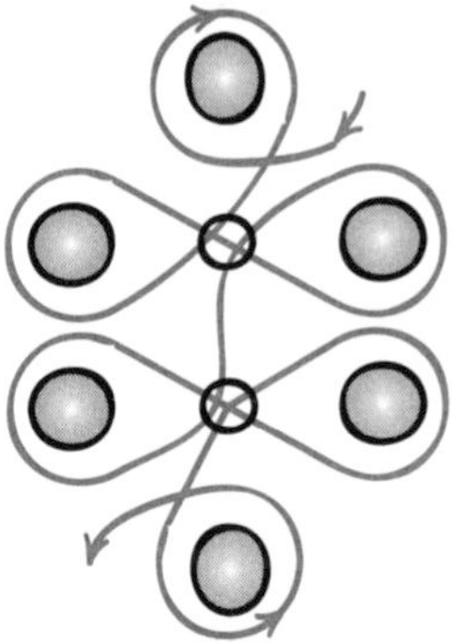

Make the Pendant

1. Arrange medium pegs on the jig in the Celtic knot pattern pictured above.
2. Place the 8¼-inch length of 18-gauge wire horizontally beneath the top peg, with 1½ inches of wire protruding from one side.
3. Hold the wire tail against the jig surface with one hand as you create the Celtic knot pattern with the wire.
4. Remove the wire from the jig.
5. Create a matching spiral on the other end of the connector, facing the opposite direction to the first.
6. Using the 26-gauge wire, convert all four briolettes into wrapped drops.
7. Use jump rings to attach the two dark natural agate briolette drops and the carnelian drop to the lower portion of the pendant, as shown.
8. Attach the bail by securing the upper spiral of the pendant to the small loop on the bail, and slip the loop of the pale carnelian drop onto the small loop of the bail before closing it.

Assemble the Necklace

1. Align the three strands of organza ribbon.
2. Attach an end cone to one end of the strands by using the 20-gauge wire to make an eye pin.
3. String the bail over all three strands of ribbon.
4. Attach the second end cone to the other end of the ribbons, making sure that all three ribbons are equal in length.
5. Attach the S-hook and clasp eye to the ends of the necklace using the 4.5mm jump rings.

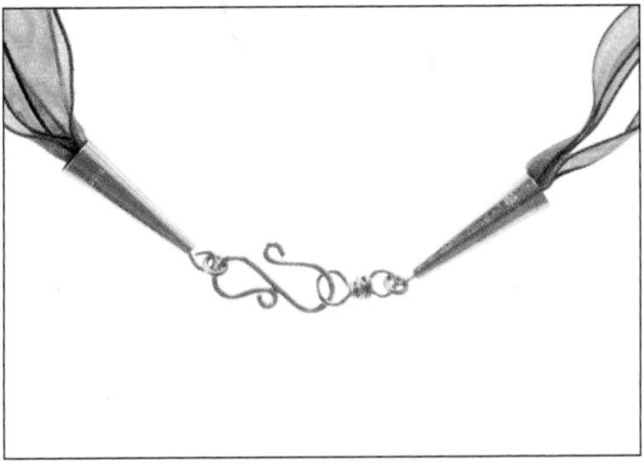

Gothic Bead Lace Collar Necklace

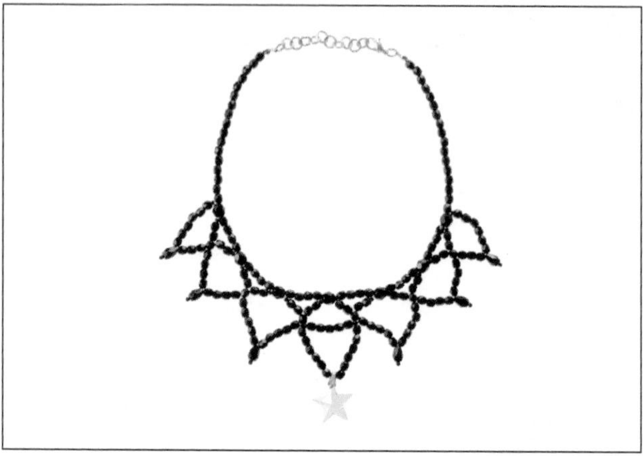

This project uses an embellished beaded lace pattern and Czech glass fire polish beads for a draped, romantic look. This design is called a collar necklace because it is very short and is worn against the neck. If you'd like to make it longer, simply increase the number of 4mm beads you string on at the beginning and end of the upper strand. And if Gothic is not your style, you can replicate the design using beads in more vibrant colors.

Length: Adjusts from about 12½ inches to 14 inches

Tools and Supplies

- Size #10 beading needle
- Sharp scissors or nippers
- Masking tape
- E6000 glue

Materials

- 23-inch length of conditioned size B beading thread in black
- 1½-yard length of conditioned size B beading thread in black
- 101 round Czech glass fire polish beads in black (4mm)
- 7 Czech glass fire polish beads in black (6mm)
- 6 faceted teardrop Czech glass fire polish beads in black (7mm x 5mm)
- 26 size 11/0 Czech seed beads in black
- Crystal star pendant in golden shadow (20mm)
- Silver-tone prong bail
- 2 silver-tone clamshell bead tips
- 12 silver-tone jump rings, 18 gauge (5mm outside diameter)
- Silver-tone lobster clasp

Make the Necklace

1. Attach the bail to the star pendant by inserting the prongs into either side of the pendant hole and squeezing them closed with your fingers.
2. Set the pendant aside.
3. Align one end of the 23-inch strand of thread with one end of the 1½-yard strand.

Gothic Bead Lace Collar Necklace *(continued)*

4. Tie two double overhand knots, one on top of the other, with both strands about 1 inch from the ends.
5. String a bead tip onto both strands, and use the glue to secure it over the knots.
6. Thread the needle onto the upper strand of thread, and fold over a few inches of thread so that you can hold it on the needle with your fingers.
7. String on 17 4mm beads and one 6mm bead.
8. String on four more 4mm beads and another 6mm bead.

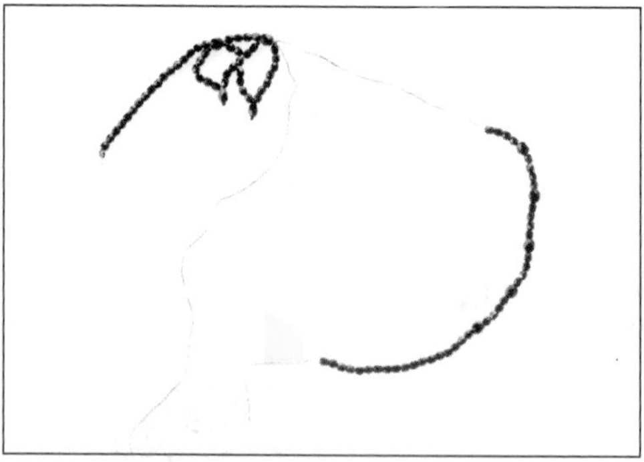

9. Repeat Step 6 five more times.
10. String on 17 4mm beads to complete the upper strand.
11. Remove the needle and tape off the end of the upper strand about 3 inches past the final bead.
12. Thread the needle onto the lower strand of thread.
13. String through the first 18 beads in the upper row.
14. Bring the needle out again and pull the thread taut.
15. String on one seed bead and six 4mm beads.
16. String on one teardrop bead and another seed bead.
17. Pull the thread taut again, and string back up through the teardrop bead.
18. String on six more 4mm beads and another seed bead.

19. String back through the next bead on the top row and out again, and pull the first lace loop taut.
20. Slide over the beads in the top row that are to the right of the bead you strung through in Step 17, and tie an overhand knot around the top strand of thread to secure the first loop.

NOTE: *Use the needle to help position the knot.*

21. Slide back the upper beads, and continue the design by following the pattern below, tying an overhand knot around the upper strand after you complete each lace loop.

NOTE: *Before you string on the pendant, string on two seed beads to support the bail.*

22. When you reach the center drop, first string the shorter loop (1 in the pattern below) then string up to the top and back down again to create the longer one (2 in the pattern below).
23. When all of the lace loops are complete, string back through the last 17 beads in the upper strand.
24. Carefully remove the tape from the top strand.
25. Finish both thread ends with a single bead tip like you did in Step 5, using the needle to help you position the final knots inside the bead tip.
26. Attach the lobster clasp to one of the bead tips using jump rings.
27. Connect the rest of the jump rings to make the extender chain, and attach it to the other bead tip.

Gothic Bead Lace Collar Necklace *(continued)*

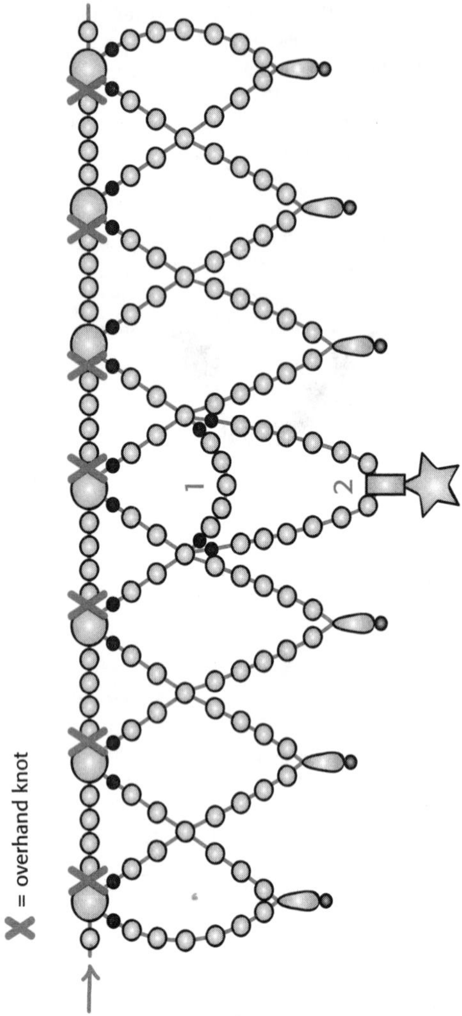

Earrings

Here are three very different earring projects—one simple single-bead design, one that involves making chain from jump rings, and one that uses bead-weaving techniques.

Cosmic Crystal Drop Earrings

Simple bead-drop earrings are especially easy to make. This design uses handmade eye pins, pre-made hooks, and funky cosmic crystal beads for a high-fashion, designer look.

You can alter the basic design of these earrings by using more elaborate head pins, like paddles and spirals. To add more beads, use an eye pin instead of a head pin, and attach one or more additional bead drops to its loop.

Tools

- Side cutters
- Round nose pliers
- Chain nose pliers
- Flat nose pliers (or a second pair of chain nose pliers)
- Chasing hammer
- Bench block

Materials

- 2 sterling-silver lever-back earring findings
- 2 sterling-silver jump rings, 18 gauge (4.5mm outside diameter)
- 2½ inches of dead-soft sterling-silver wire, 20 gauge
- 2 cosmic crystal beads in indicolite (16mm)

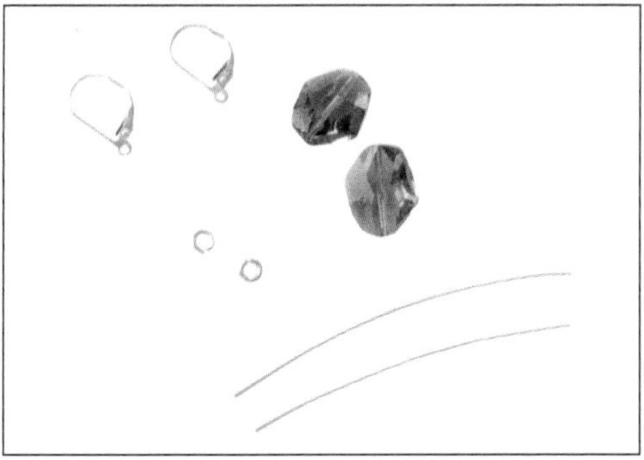

Make the Earrings

1. Cut the wire into two equal, blunt-cut lengths, each about $1\frac{1}{4}$ inches.
2. Use chain nose pliers to fold over one end of each wire length to create simple head pins.

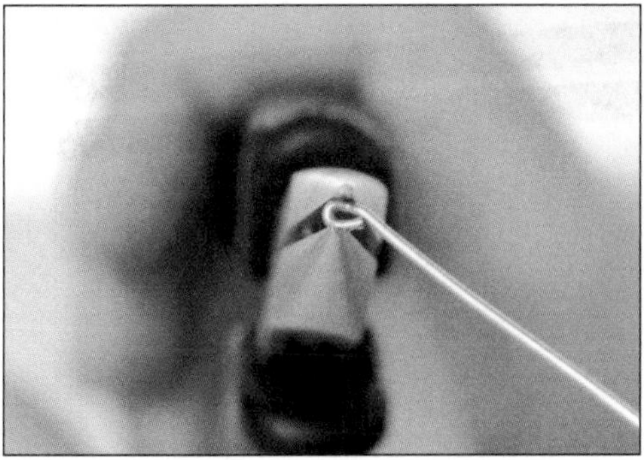

Cosmic Crystal Drop Earrings
(continued)

3. Place a bead on each head pin.

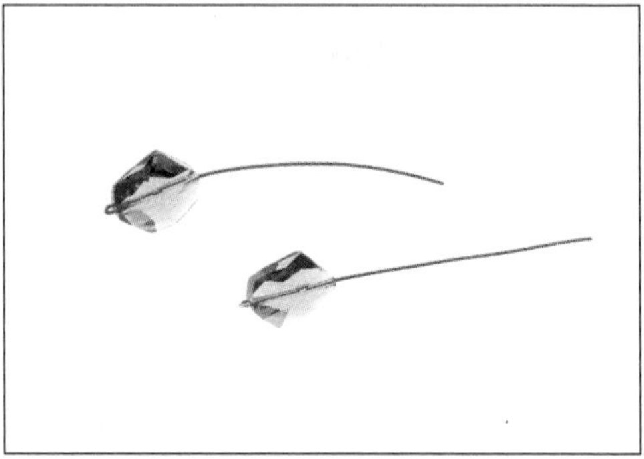

4. Use round nose pliers to create a simple loop at the top of each bead. Trim off the excess wire.
5. Use both pairs of pliers to open the jump rings.
6. Place a bead drop and earring finding on each jump ring and close it securely.

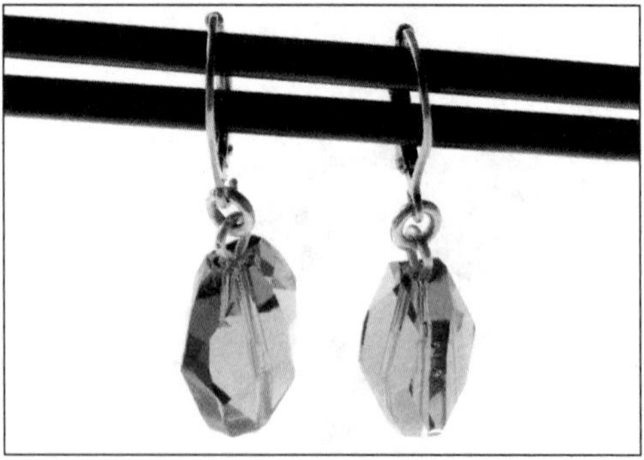

Byzantine and Turquoise Drop Earrings

The Byzantine chain is usually used in bracelets and necklaces, but you can also use it to make chunky drop earrings. In this design, a short length of sterling-silver Byzantine chain is accented by a turquoise cube bead drop.

Tools and Supplies

- Chain nose pliers
- Flat nose pliers
- Side cutters
- Chasing hammer
- Bench block
- Needle file
- Safety pin

Materials

- 28 sterling-silver jump rings, 18 gauge (5.5mm outside diameter)
- 2 sterling-silver jump rings, 18 gauge (4mm outside diameter)
- 2 wirework earring hooks made from 22-gauge sterling-silver wire
- 2 natural blue turquoise beads (6mm)
- Two ⅞-inch lengths of 20-gauge dead-soft sterling-silver wire

Byzantine and Turquoise Drop Earrings *(continued)*

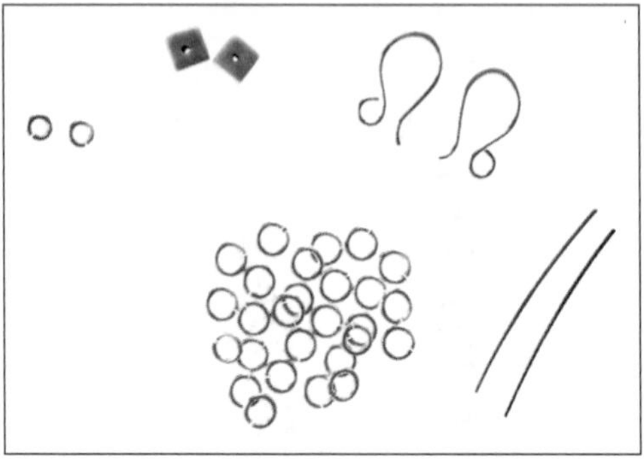

TIP

Byzantine chain uses a large number of jump rings. You will use up jump rings quickly, so consider purchasing pre-made rings in bulk, or invest in equipment for making jump rings if you enjoy this technique.

Make Byzantine Chain

1. Place two closed jump rings on a safety pin.
2. After closing the safety pin, slip an open jump ring through both closed rings, and close it.
3. Repeat Step 2 to add a second closed jump ring to the original two rings.

4. Using the same procedure, add two more jump rings to the two rings that you added in steps 2–3. You now have a three-link chain of double jump rings.

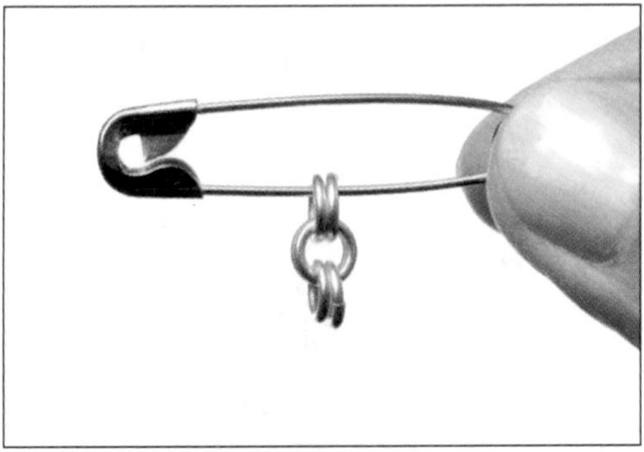

5. Grip the first two links of the chain (four rings total) with the fingers of one hand.
6. Fold back the last two rings in the chain so that they fall to opposite sides.
7. Add the two folded-back rings to the rings you're holding in your fingers.

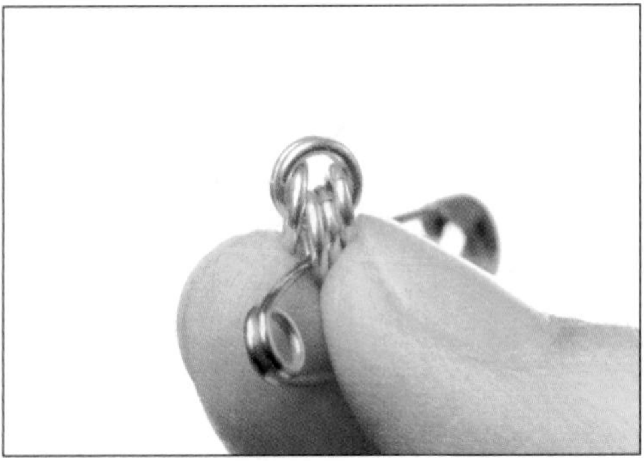

Byzantine and Turquoise Drop Earrings *(continued)*

8 Fold back the next two rings at the end of the chain as far as they will go. This will expose the next set of two rings below (shown in blue).

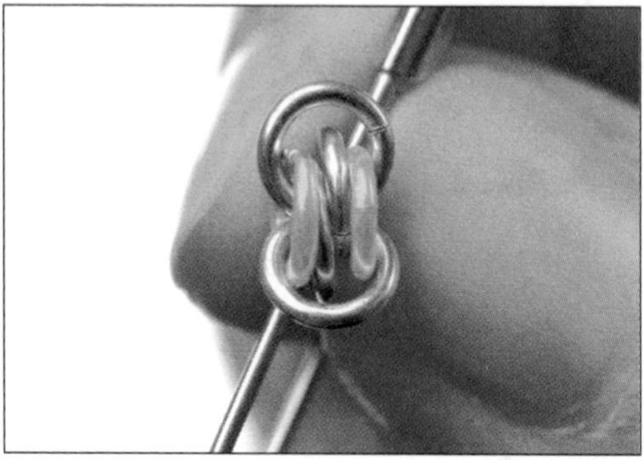

9 While still holding the chain with one hand, use flat nose pliers in your other hand to thread a new open jump ring through the two lower rings that are now exposed.

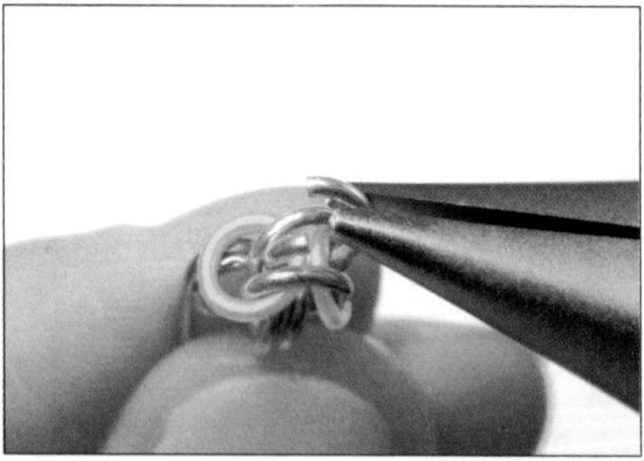

⑩ Add a second closed jump ring to those two lower rings. The chain should look like this.

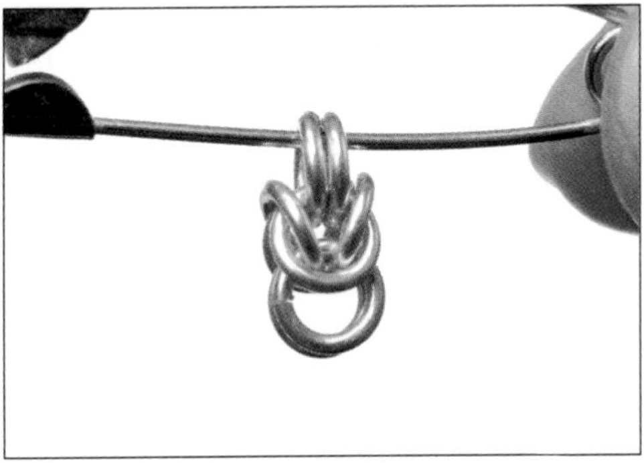

⑪ Attach two more links of two jump rings each to the rings that you added in Step 10. The chain should look like this.

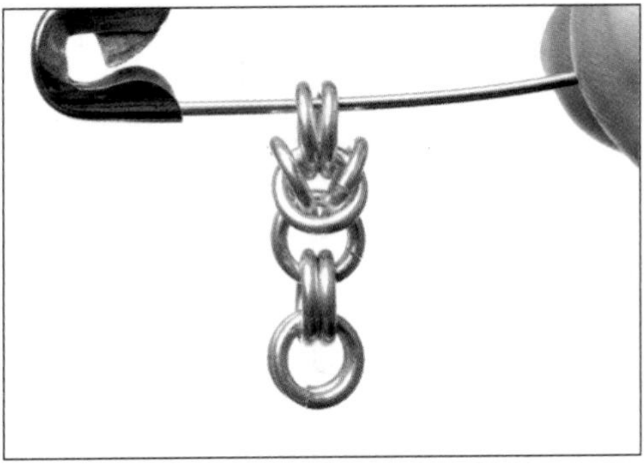

Byzantine and Turquoise Drop Earrings *(continued)*

12. Fold back the last two rings so that they fall to the sides, as you did in Step 6.
13. Fold back the next two rings as far as they will go, exposing the next two rings between them.
14. Repeat steps 9–13 until you have the desired length of chain.

Make the Earrings

1. Use both sets of pliers, the safety pin, and the 28 6mm jump rings to create two lengths of Byzantine chain containing 14 jump rings each, as shown.

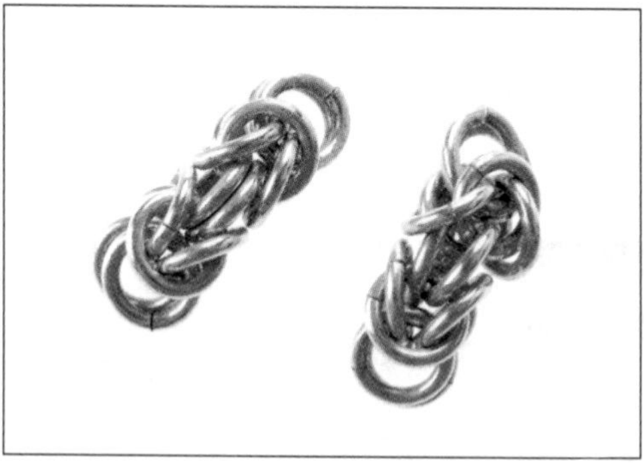

2. Connect the top two rings in each length of chain to each earring hook using the two 4mm jump rings.
3. Use the hammer and bench block to convert each of the ⅞-inch lengths of 20-gauge wire into paddle head pins.

❹ Smooth the edges of the paddles using the needle file.

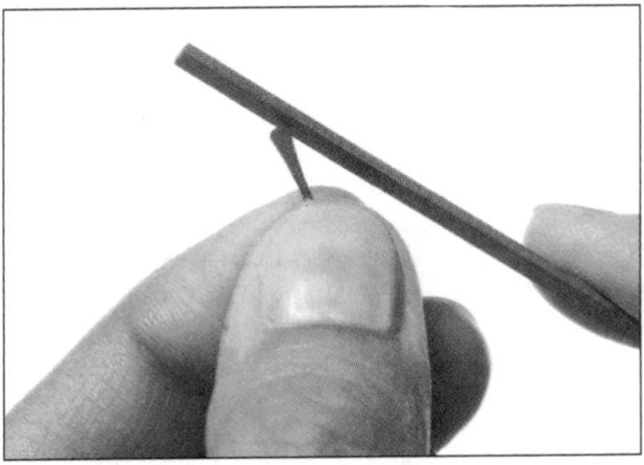

❺ String each turquoise bead onto each head pin.

Byzantine and Turquoise Drop Earrings *(continued)*

6. Use the side cutters to trim each head pin about ¼ inch above each bead. (Be sure to make blunt cuts.)
7. Use round nose pliers to create a loop above the bead on each head pin.
8. Attach each head-pin loop directly to the bottom two rings in each of the Byzantine chains.

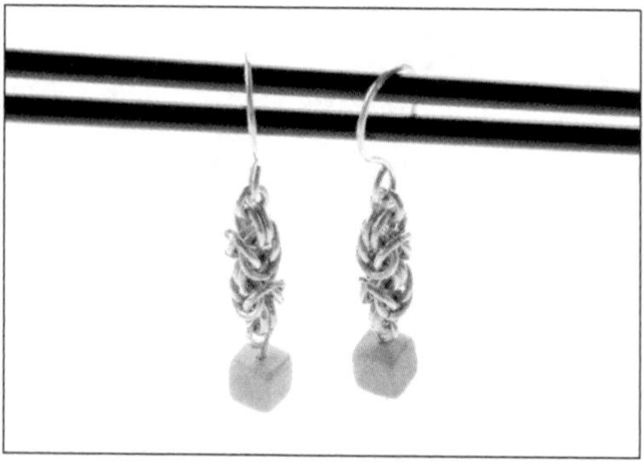

TIP

Many beginner jewelry makers become frustrated when they find themselves scratching and marring wire with their pliers. You may not always be able to avoid scratching your wire, but you can take measures to reduce the occurrence and severity of scratches.

An easy way is to cover the jaws of your pliers with a layer or two of masking tape. It will need to be replaced from time to time, and more often when you're working with larger-gauge wire.

Another option is to use a special tool-liquid product designed to coat the jaws of your pliers with a layer of soft plastic. You can purchase these products from the larger jewelry supply retailers. Typically, you need to dip your pliers into the liquid, and then hang them up to dry.

Netting and Right-Angle Weave Earrings

These colorful earrings begin with right-angle weave tops that serve as decorative bases for fans of vertical netting. Keep a close eye on the patterns as you work to make sure that you pick up beads in the proper number and sequence. If the multicolor pattern seems daunting, try them in a single color first for practice.

Tools and Supplies

- Beading scissors
- Thread conditioner or beeswax
- Bead dishes and/or bead mat
- Ruler or measuring tape
- Size 13 beading needle

Netting and Right-Angle Weave Earrings *(continued)*

Materials

- Size D Nymo beading thread in olive
- 2 gold-filled French hook earring findings
- 1 gram size 15/0 Japanese seed beads in opaque medium orange (A)
- 1 gram size 15/0 Japanese seed beads in transparent matte tourmaline (B)
- 1 gram size 15/0 Japanese seed beads in opaque dark orange (C)
- .5 gram size 11/0 Japanese seed beads in opaque medium green (D)
- .5 gram size 15/0 Japanese seed beads in shimmering icy green (E)

NOTE: *Bead weights are rounded up to the nearest .5 gram.*

Stitch the Flat Right-Angle Weave

1. String four beads onto your thread.
2. Bring the thread back around and tie a square knot at the base of the first bead. You now have a tiny loop of four beads.

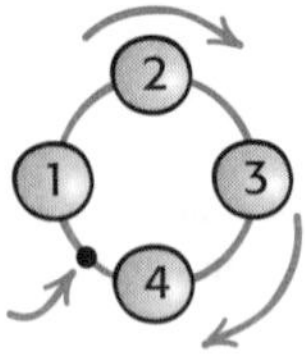

3. Thread into the first bead again, in the same direction.
4. Thread through the next two beads and out again.
5. String on three more beads.
6. Thread back down into the third bead that you strung on in Step 1 from top to bottom.
7. Thread back through the first two beads that you strung on in Step 4 and out again.
8. String on three more beads.
9. Thread back up into the second bead that you strung on in Step 4.

⑩ Thread through the next two beads and out again.

⑪ Continue adding groups of three beads until you have a row of the desired length with the thread pointing up.

NOTE: *The thread alternates between pointing up and pointing down with each stitch. The last stitch in any row should be the type that leaves the thread pointing up.*

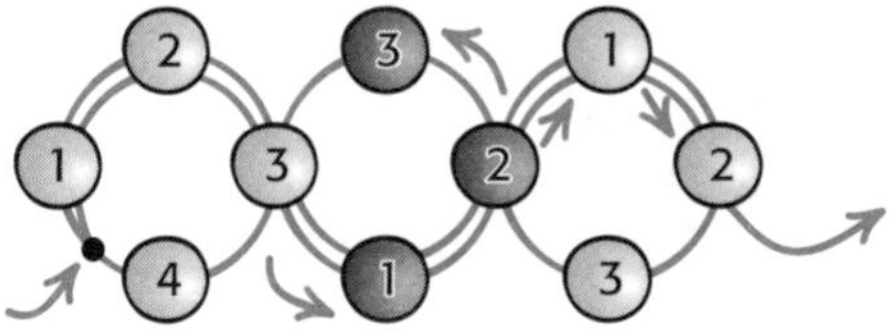

⑫ To begin the next row, thread back into the last upper bead in the row.

⑬ String on three more beads.

⑭ Thread down into the last upper bead in the previous row again, then back through the first bead from Step 13 one more time.

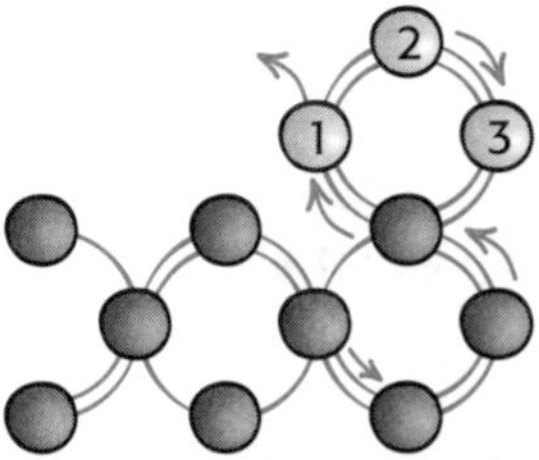

⑮ Turn your work around and string on two more beads (beads 4 and 5).

⑯ Thread down through the next upper bead of the previous row and back up through the first bead from Step 13.

⑰ Thread back into the two beads from Step 15.

⑱ Thread down through the next upper bead of the previous row and out again.

⑲ String on two more beads.

20 Continue creating figure-eight loops to the end of the row, and continue stitching rows back and forth to the desired length.

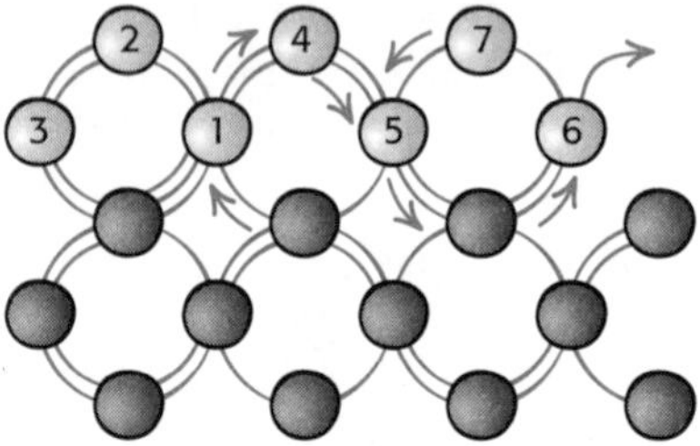

Make the Earring Tops

1. Prepare a length of thread that is about $1\frac{1}{2}$ times as long as your arm span, without a bead stop.
2. After threading the needle, pick up four beads for the first unit of flat right-angle weave, reading the pattern below from the bottom-left corner and moving in a clockwise direction around the first unit. (The first bead to pick up is labeled 1.)

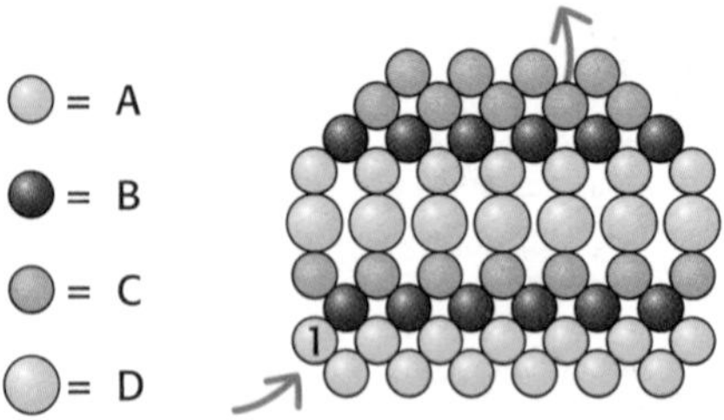

3. Position the beads about 2 feet from the needle end of the thread. (The extra-long tail is used later for the netting.)
4. Follow the pattern to stitch the first two unit rows of beadwork. The first unit row is regular right-angle weave, and the second is multiple-bead right-angle weave (the tops and bottoms of each unit contain one bead each, and the sides contain sets of the three beads each).

5 Begin the third unit row with an outside decrease. You should not need to weave through the beadwork to change the location of the thread; simply pass back through the second from last high bead in the previous row, which is marked with an asterisk in the pattern. (The first three beads that you pick up for the first unit of the third row are labeled 1, 2, and 3.)

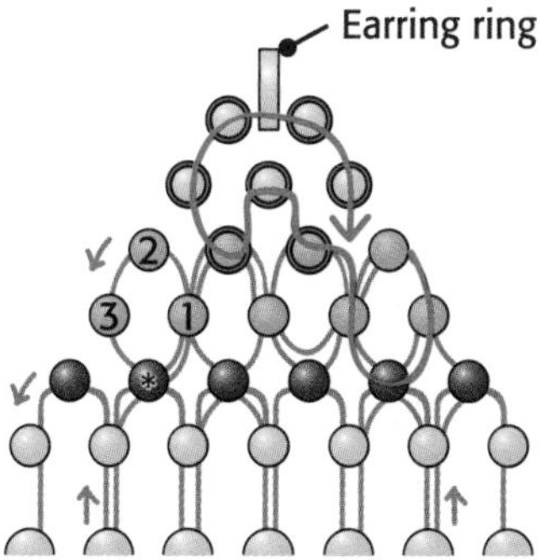

6 Complete the third unit row with an outside decrease by stopping one unit earlier than the end of the previous row.

7 Create the top loop: Following the path shown in the diagram, pass through the lower three beads in the last unit of the third unit row again, and then back through the second from last high bead in the third unit row.

Netting and Right-Angle Weave Earrings *(continued)*

8. Pick up 1A and pass back through the third from last high bead in the third unit row, following the path shown in the diagram.
9. Pull the thread taut and then pick up 2A.
10. Pass the needle through the bottom ring on the earring finding and then pick up another 2A.
11. Pass through all seven beads (outlined in the diagram) that make up the loop one more time.
12. Pull the thread taut and remove the needle from the thread. (You can weave in and end the tail within the netting later.)

Vertical Netting Pattern

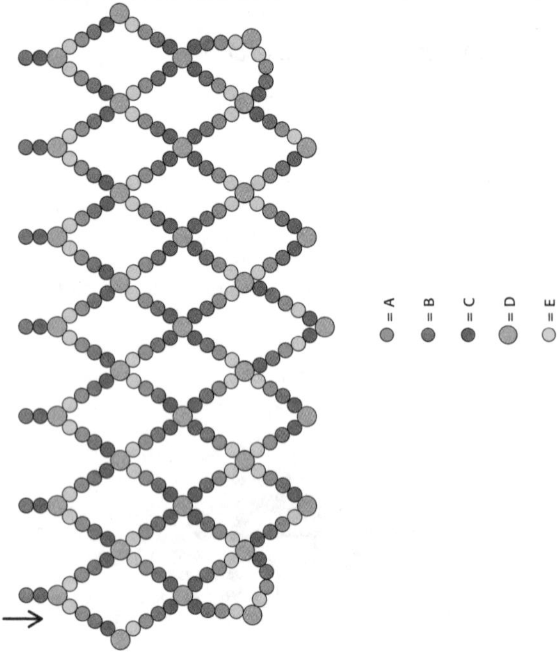

Make the Netting

1. Thread the needle onto the other end of the thread.
2. Begin the vertical netting pattern by picking up 1B, 1C, and 1D.
3. Following the pattern, stitch the first column of netting, turn, and stitch the second column of netting.
4. At the top of the second column, pass back through the 1D, 1C, and 1B that you picked up in Step 2.
5. Pull the thread taut and then pass back through the bead in the earring top that the thread initially exited.
6. Moving clockwise, pass through the next two beads in that right-angle weave unit and pull the thread taut.
7. Following the pattern, stitch the next two columns of vertical netting. Begin by picking up 1B, 1C, and 1D. Pass back through those beads when you arrive back at the top of the netting.

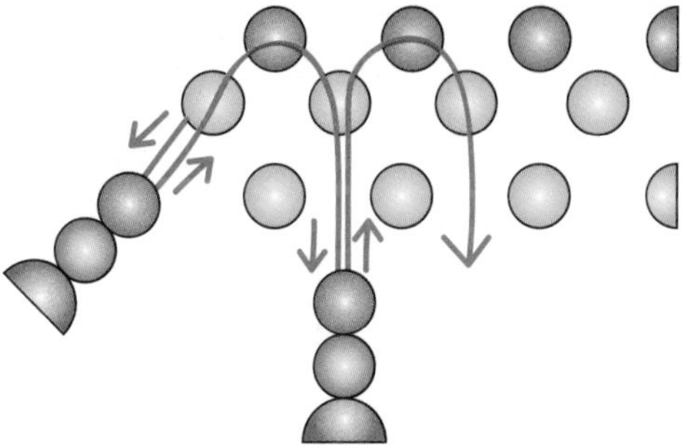

8. Using this same process, and following the pattern, stitch all of the vertical netting.
9. When the netting is complete, pass back into the earring top, reverse direction, and then pass down into the netting.
10. End the thread within a column of netting by weaving in with knots.

Netting and Right-Angle Weave Earrings *(continued)*

11. Go back to the first thread tail and weave it through the earring top toward the netting.
12. End the second tail by weaving into one of the netting columns. Be sure to select a different column than the one you used to weave-in the first thread tail.

TIP

Stitching vertical netting with proper tension takes practice. The goal is to produce beadwork that is loose enough not to curl or twist, but tight enough that no more thread than necessary shows between beads. Don't get discouraged if your tension isn't perfect at first; it will become more even with practice.

The lower loops of these earrings intentionally ruffle because they are larger than the upper loops. Even if you keep tight thread tension, the ruffles are relatively soft. To make them stiffer, you can weave back through all the netting (following the path of existing thread), using size B or size 0 thread. Be sure to end this reinforcement thread within the netting rather than within the earring top, which is already passed through many times.

Rings

Rings are fun little projects because they come together quickly and can add a lot of bling to your look. In this chapter, you'll find a couple of simple wirework rings, along with two beaded rings.

Simple Wrapped Ring

You can use wirework skills to create beautiful, stylish rings that don't require solder or molten metal. Here's a simple all-wire design.

Tools

- Ring mandrel with size markings
- Pliers (optional)
- Side cutters

Materials

- 10-inch length of 16-gauge wire

Make the Ring

1. Center the wire across the ring mandrel, aligned with the mark for one half-size larger than you would like the finished ring to be.
2. Holding the wire against the mandrel with the thumb of one hand, use your other hand to bend back both ends of wire behind the mandrel.

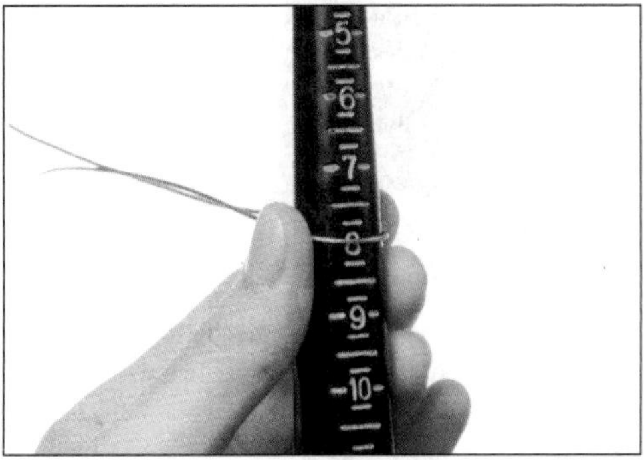

3. Pass both wires around the back of the mandrel, but do not allow them to cross over one another. (They should remain parallel.)

4. While continuing to hold the wire in place on the mandrel, bend the wire back around to the front of the mandrel and cross them past one another there.

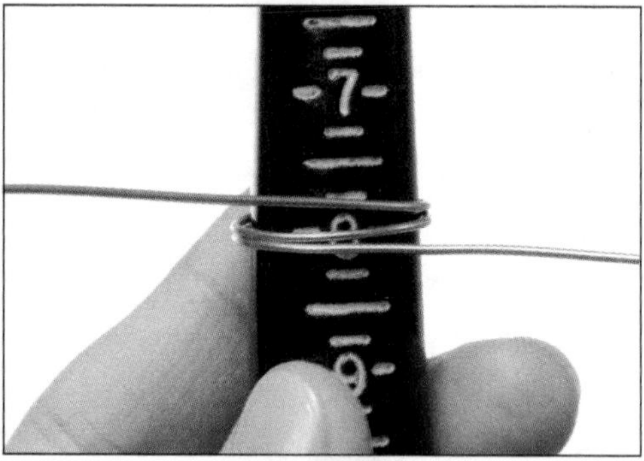

5. Bend the upper wire down over the lower two wires.
6. Bend the bottom wire up over the upper two wires.

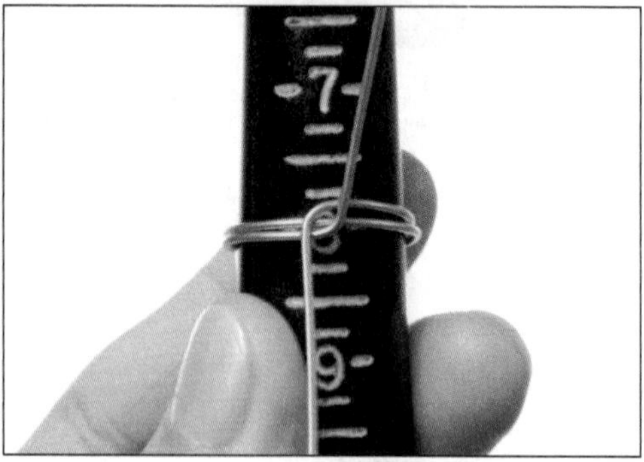

7. Remove the wire from the mandrel.
8. Using your fingers or pliers, wrap each wire end around the ring two or three times, wrapping outward from the center of the ring.
9. Trim off the excess wire and flatten down the ends with chain nose pliers.

TIP

A ring mandrel with size markings is useful for making rings of particular sizes, but it's not a foolproof tool. Notice that you made the simple wrapped ring by wrapping it one-half size larger than its finished size. This is to accommodate the added thickness of the heavy-gauge wire that you wrapped around the band in later steps. (It makes the inside circumference of the ring slightly smaller than it was at first.)

Keep this in mind when you design your own rings. Any wire wrapped around the ring's band will decrease its size to some degree. Even some large beads, if they sit low enough in the ring, may change its inside circumference. Keep your sized ring mandrel on hand when you experiment with new designs, and make note of any significant size changes that you experience during the process.

Wrapped Bead Ring

Try wrapping a beaded ring. If you like the results, you can experiment with different wraps and embellishments.

Tools

- Ring mandrel
- Chain nose pliers
- Side cutters

Materials

- 15-inch length of 20-gauge wire
- Small or medium-sized round bead

Make the Ring

1. String the bead onto the wire and center it along the wire.
2. Bend up both ends of the wire on either side of the bead.

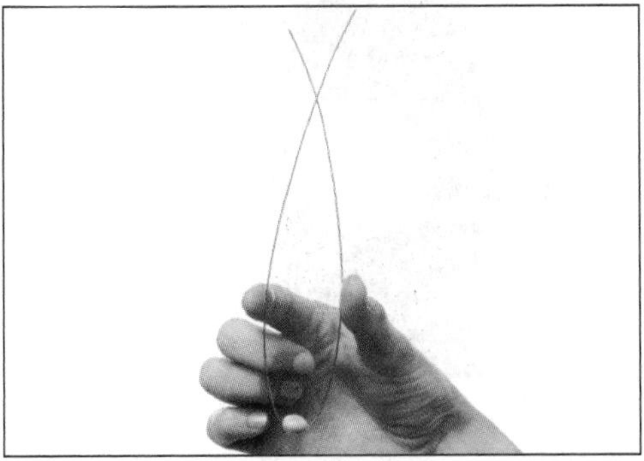

3. Place the bead against the ring mandrel at the size mark you would like the finished ring to measure, with the wire ends positioned toward the back of the mandrel.

NOTE: *Some ring mandrels have a channel on one side in which the bead can rest to help hold it in place.*

4. Cross the wire ends past one another against the back of the mandrel.
5. Bring both wires around to the front of the mandrel.

6. Position the wires so that each wraps slightly under the edge of the bead (between the bead and the mandrel).

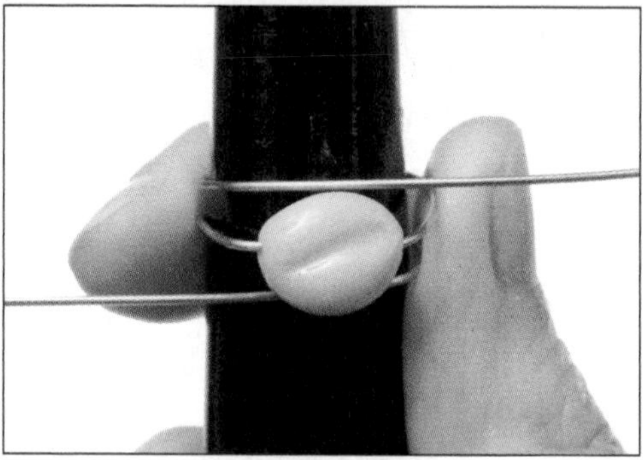

7. Bend the lower wire up against the side of the bead and over the wire that goes through the bead hole.

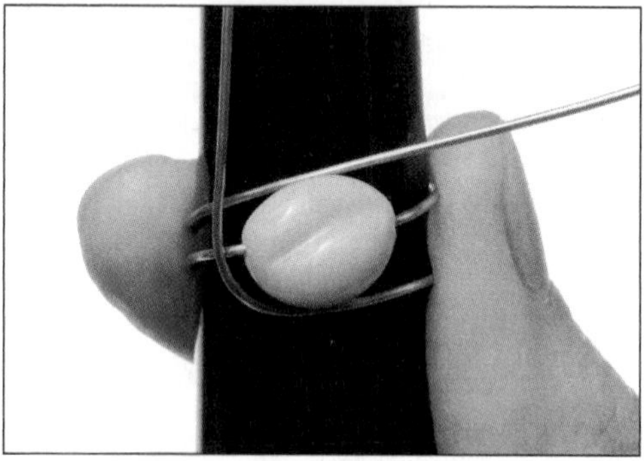

8 Wrap this wire completely around the bead one time.

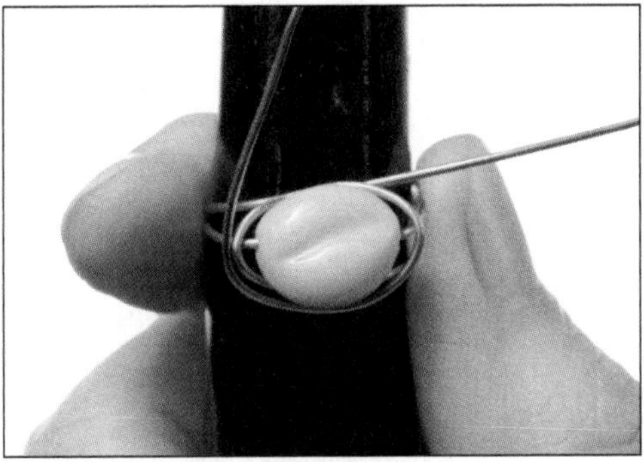

9 Bend the upper wire down against the other side of the bead.

10 Wrap that wire completely around the bead one time. The two wires should now point in opposite directions at either side of the bead.

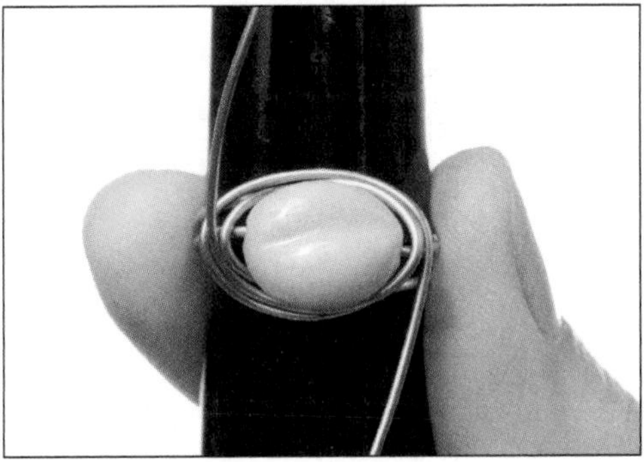

Wrapped Bead Ring *(continued)*

11. Remove the ring from the mandrel.
12. Using your fingers or chain nose pliers, wrap the wire on the left side of the ring down behind the ring band.
13. Wrap this wire securely around the band about three times.

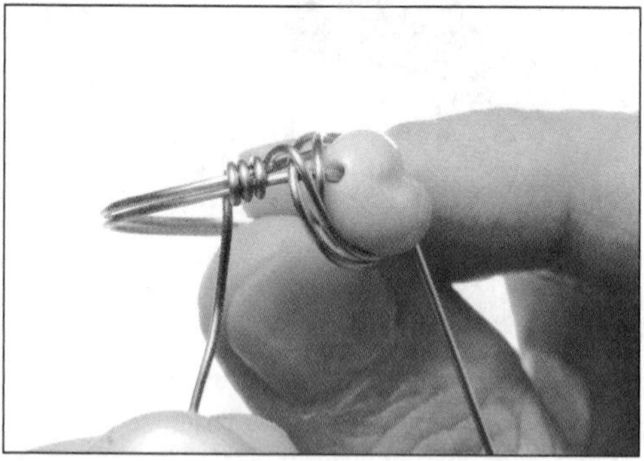

14. Using the same technique, wrap the wire on the right side of the ring around the band on that side.
15. Trim off the extra wire from both sides, and flatten down the wire ends using chain nose pliers.

Memory Wire and Crystal Heart Finger Ring

This fun, casual finger ring features crystal components and small coils of memory wire. A crystal heart setting and beads in topaz and clear crystal are used here, but you can find similar settings and beads in a variety of colors and shapes.

Tools and Supplies

- 2 small alligator clamps
- Memory wire cutters (or heavy-duty household wire cutters)
- E6000 glue
- Paper towels
- Round nose pliers

Materials

- 2 full, separate coils of finger-ring-sized silver-tone memory wire
- 20 faceted crystal round beads in light Colorado topaz (3mm)
- 4 faceted crystal round beads in smoked topaz (4mm)
- 4 faceted crystal round beads in clear (5mm)
- 4 round silver-plate memory wire end caps (3mm)
- Double-hole Swarovski crystal heart setting in clear
- 2 blunt-cut ⅝-inch lengths of 20-gauge silver-tone wire

Memory Wire and Crystal Heart Finger Ring *(continued)*

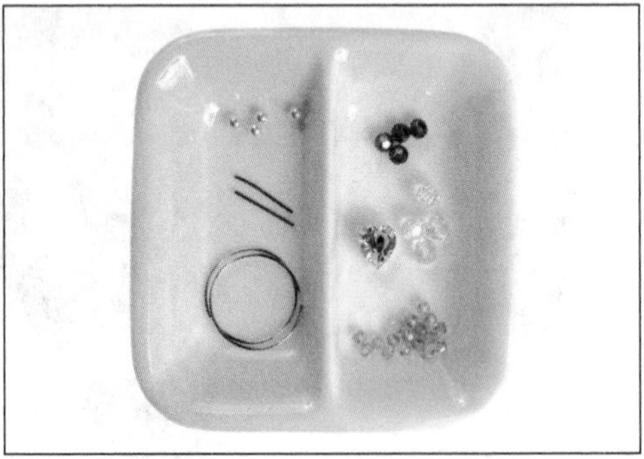

Make the Ring

1. Glue an end cap onto one end of each of the two memory wire coils, and allow the glue to fully set.
2. String four Colorado topaz beads onto each coil.
3. Use the round nose pliers to create a figure eight–shaped simple clasp eye using one length of the 20-gauge wire. Make both loops very small and the same size. This component will serve as a spacer bar.
4. String one loop of the spacer bar onto one of the memory wire coils.
5. String the other loop of the spacer bar onto the other memory wire coil.
6. String another Colorado topaz bead onto each coil.
7. String one smoked topaz bead and one clear bead onto each coil.

8. Thread one coil through the two top holes in the crystal heart setting.
9. Thread the other coil through the two bottom holes in the crystal heart setting.
10. String two clear beads onto each coil, against the heart component.
11. String one smoked topaz bead and one Colorado topaz bead onto each coil.
12. Create a second separator bar with the remaining length of 20-gauge wire, and string it onto both coils.
13. String four more Colorado topaz beads onto each coil.
14. Attach an alligator clamp to each coil after stringing on the final bead.
15. Finish both coils by gluing on the remaining end caps.
16. When the glue has set, remove the alligator clamps.

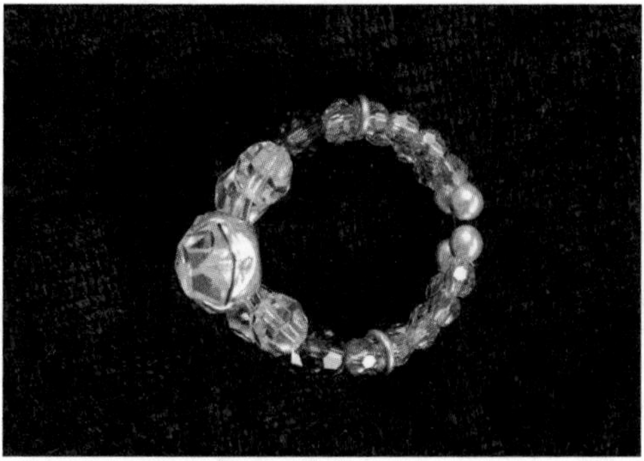

Even-Count Flat Peyote Stitch Finger Ring

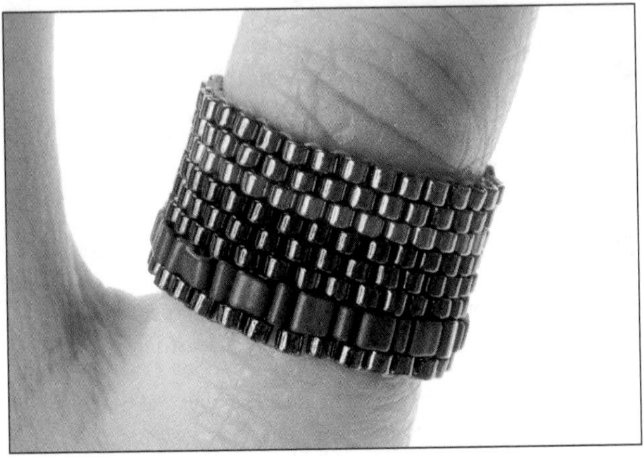

The even-count flat peyote stitch creates a smooth, flat, beaded fabric that is perfect for making finger rings. The basic technique involves stitching together the ends of the fabric to make a beaded tube. You can use this method to make just about any width of finger ring that you would like, as long as you complete the fabric with an even number of rows.

Tools and Supplies

- Sharp scissors or nippers
- Size 11 beading needle
- Thread conditioner

Materials

- 1⅕ yards of conditioned size B beading thread in gold
- 82 size 11/0 cylinder beads in metallic bronze
- 41 size 11/0 cylinder beads in metallic light bronze
- 123 size 11/0 cylinder beads in metallic olive
- 41 size 11/0 Japanese triangle seed beads in matte metallic dark brown
- 41 size 11/0 cylinder beads in metallic hematite

Pattern

- Metallic hematite
- Matte metallic dark brown
- Metallic olive
- Metallic light bronze
- Metallic bronze

Even-Count Flat Peyote Stitch Finger Ring *(continued)*

Weave the Even-Count Flat Peyote Stitch

1. String on an even number of beads to equal the width that you'd like your finished design to be.
2. String on one more bead.
3. String back through the last bead that you strung on in Step 1 in the opposite direction.

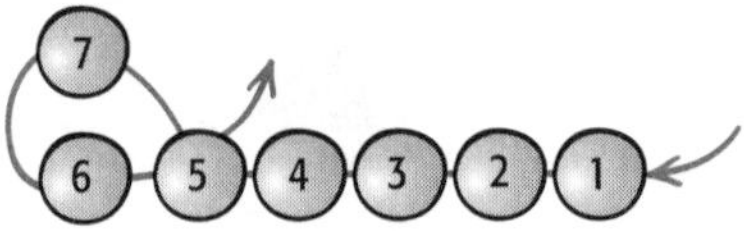

4. Turn your work around and string on another bead.
5. String back through the fourth from the last bead that you strung on in Step 1 (Bead 8).

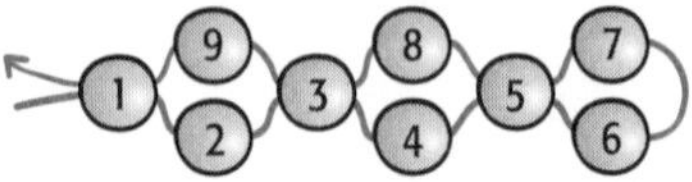

6. Continue adding a new bead and stringing through a lower bead until you arrive back at the beginning of the first row. String back through the first bead that you strung on in Step 1.
7. Turn your work again and string on a new bead (Bead 10).
8. String back through the first bead in the second row (Bead 9).

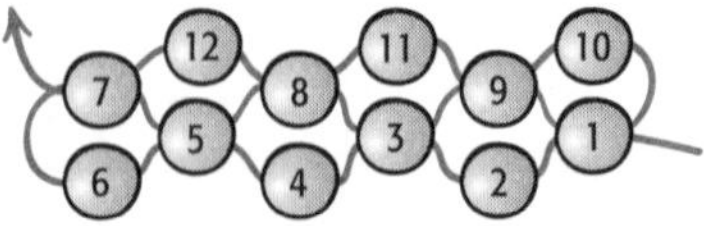

9. Continue this pattern, stitching each row in the opposite direction to the prior row.

Make the Ring

1. Thread the needle onto the conditioned beading thread, and fold over the first few inches of thread so that you can weave using a single strand of thread.
2. String on and secure a stop bead about 6 inches from the end of the thread.
3. String on one hematite bead, one dark brown triangle bead, three olive beads, one light bronze bead, and two bronze beads.

NOTE: *Feel free to change the order of the colors to vary the look.*

4. Slide all eight beads up against the stop bead.
5. String on another bronze bead and thread back through the second-to-last bronze bead in the first row to complete the second row of even-count peyote stitch.
6. Weave each successive row using even-count flat peyote stitch (see above for general instructions).
7. After finishing the final row, tie an overhand knot around the nearest woven thread.
8. Bring the two sides of beaded fabric together and stitch them in a zigzag pattern, back and forth through each protruding bead on either side of the fabric. (The sides will come together like a zipper.)

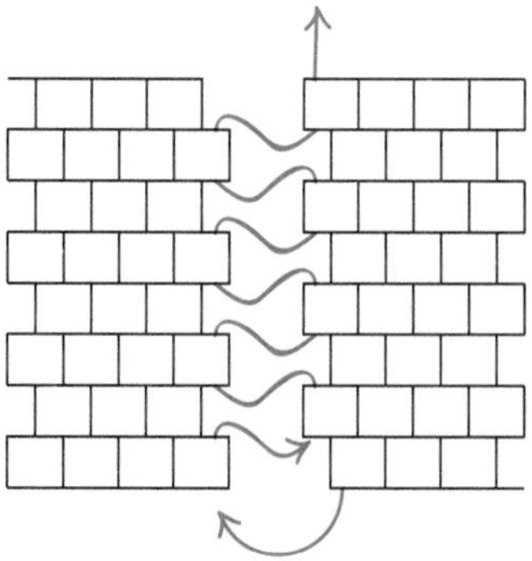

Even-Count Flat Peyote Stitch Finger Ring *(continued)*

9. To secure the seam, zigzag stitch back down through a few more beads, and then weave in your thread as usual.
10. Remove the stop bead from the beginning end of thread and use the needle to weave in that thread as well.